Are You Managing?

ALLIED DUNBAR

Are You Managing?

by
Peter Stemp

THE INDUSTRIAL SOCIETY

First published 1988 by
The Industrial Society
Peter Runge House
3 Carlton House Terrace
London
SW1Y 5DG

ISBN 0 85290 3995

Illustrations by Larry

British Library Cataloguing in Publications Data

Stemp, Peter

Are You Managing?
1. Management - Manuals
I. Title II. Allied Dunbar III. Industrial Society
658.4

Allied Dunbar Assurance plc
Allied Dunbar Centre
Swindon SN1 1EL
Tel: 0793 514514

Whilst every care has been taken in the compilation of this book, please bear in mind that certain employment situations will require the advice of specialists in the field of employment law.

ACKNOWLEDGEMENT

Like most tasks in life, real achievement can only be attained as a result of successful teamwork by many individuals. At times I am sure there was a cast of thousands involved in producing this work and I'm sure I will offend somebody by omitting their name. However, I would particularly like to acknowledge the contribution made by Keith Davies, Richard McGonigle, Clyde Nancarrow, John Rushworth, Peter Steggall, George Wilson, Stephen Wigzell and John Williams and in addition to Bob Gill, Clifford Green and Sally Randles who have helped with the production of this book.

Peter Stemp
Personnel Director
Allied Dunbar Assurance plc

FOREWORD

Good management is very often the application of common-sense, but sometimes commonsense needs pointing out so that we can all recognise it. "Are You Managing?" is a handbook of commonsense management written in a straightforward and practical way for busy managers.

Most people need to refresh their memories every now and again about good practice and this book is full of sound advice about how to apply good practice in the real world.

As we strive to improve our nation's competitive edge we need continually to improve our self management and our leadership of others. Those managers who apply the principles from this book to their everyday work will be well on their way to achieving these improvements.

Alistair Graham
Director
The Industrial Society

CONTENTS

1 **Managing Yourself**   **1**
 Understand yourself
 Manage effectively
 Delegate
 Checklist 1

2 **Managing Others**   **17**
 Lead by example
 Build working relationships
 Manage for results
 Checklist 2

3 **Managing Your Boss**   **35**
 Checklist 3

4 **Managing Performance**   **41**
 Plan performance
 Track performance
 Stay informed
 Improve performance
 Appraise performance
 Checklist 4

5 **Managing Discipline and Grievances**   **57**
 Discipline fairly
 Avoid grievances
 Checklist 5

6 **Managing Recruitment**   **67**
 Checklist 6

7 Managing Reward   **75**
Recognise contribution
Reward fairly
Checklist 7

8 Managing Training and Development   **81**
Provide proper training
Support individual development
Checklist 8

9 Managing Communication   **95**
Develop your communication skills
Keep others informed
Keep yourself in touch
Manage meetings
Checklist 9

10 Managing Organisation   **107**
Develop an appropriate structure
Build teams and teamwork
Aim for organisational effectiveness
Checklist 10

11 Managing Quality   **119**
Set clear standards
Achieve the standards
Track the quality achieved
Improve quality
Checklist 11

12 Managing Productivity   **129**
Focus on productivity
Plan to be productive
Ensure performance is productive
Maximise productivity
Checklist 12

INDEX   **144**

1 MANAGING YOURSELF

This is where effective management begins. When you manage yourself well, you are in a better position to achieve through others.

There are three essentials to Managing Yourself:

- Know yourself. As a Manager, it helps to understand how you 'tick' and are perceived.
- Be clear about your objectives and address the right priorities.
- Make sure that your personal organisation is efficient.

In a nutshell, you need to understand yourself, manage effectively and manage efficiently.

Understand yourself

By knowing your strengths, you can identify the areas in which you are likely to be able to make the best contribution. You need to understand your weaknesses and limitations (we all have them!) to be able to work at changing your behaviour and/or enlist the help of others in these areas. It is also important to know what drives your behaviour so that you are better able to control how you react in certain situations.

As a Manager, you need both physical and mental stamina in order to get results and make the difficult decisions that management requires. All of us have our own warning signs when we have been pushing ourselves too hard. Be able to recognise your own personal symptoms of stress and learn what you need to do to remain effective and in control.

Self-awareness usually increases with age and maturity but, if you can't wait that long, there are things that you can be doing.

Evaluate yourself

From time to time, review your own performance and list your strengths and weaknesses. Write down what motivates you, your talents and abilities and what you are going to do to develop yourself. Self-evaluation will allow you to play to your strengths and help you to get what you want from your job.

Seek feedback from others

Asking about yourself can be as boring to others as talking about yourself, but now and again check out other people's perception of you. Ask your team, your boss and other Managers how specific things have gone or could have been handled better, probe further on a few aspects and you'll get feedback on yourself.

Manage effectively

Effective management depends on doing the right things.

As a Manager you have a lot of discretion on how to tackle your job. You always need to be thinking very carefully about what is involved and what you should be doing. Your top priority should be to know where to concentrate your time and effort to best effect.

From time to time, step back and review how you are managing. Whatever your particular situation, it is always useful to ask yourself the following:

Evaluate Yourself

Am I clear about what I am expected to achieve?

It might seem a pretty obvious question, but it's amazing how often Managers are not exactly sure what is required or the results that they are expected to achieve. If you as the Manager aren't clear in your own mind on this, your people will also be uncertain and performance will suffer. Whilst you won't always have every detail spelt out for you, there are some essentials which you need to know:

- Who your boss is and what you are responsible for (which should be written up as an organisation chart and job description).

- Your objectives and priorities. You need to know what is expected from you and your area in terms of output, performance and the standards you should be aiming for, including quality and cost.

- What the limits of your authority are – i.e. what decisions you are entitled to take and what needs to be referred.

- What is required in terms of reporting on-going progress and developments.

If you're not sure about any of these essentials, ask your boss. It will benefit both of you to clarify things.

Have I got the right balance between doing and managing?

Whatever your level as a Manager, you will probably have a personal workload as well. That might involve doing things your subordinates do already or could learn to do. It might be necessary to help out with the workload or you may need to apply your specialist knowledge and experience on project work. However, you do need to think consciously about the right way to split your management time, remembering that:

- Doing other work shouldn't divert you from managing properly. Management is about deciding what to do and getting it done through other people – not by yourself.

- 'Doing It Yourself' can remove interest and responsibility from the jobs of your people and restrict their development.

- There is often a great temptation for Managers not to let go of their last job (either through lack of confidence in others or themselves) or spend time on favourite areas in which a special interest has been kept.

- As a general rule, the higher your level, the more time you need to spend on management (directing, planning, controlling and organising) rather than doing/producing. However, you'll still need to drop down into detail when it is appropriate.

Record how you use your time to find out if you're striking the right balance between doing and managing. Compare your own view and the perceptions of your boss and your team on whether you are spending the right amount of time on personal work, managing people and managing tasks.

Finally, remember that you are also a member of a larger management team as well as Manager of your own group. Allow time to make a contribution in this wider role.

Have I got the right emphasis between my management activities?

First, you need to know the basic activities which are involved in management. These are:

People Oriented

• Motivation	–	encouraging people to meet objectives and achieve higher levels of job performance and productivity.
• Development	–	providing opportunities for people to develop their skills, knowledge, confidence and commitment.
• Recognition	–	acknowledging and rewarding people on merit.

- Caring   –   showing respect and concern for the individual and the team.

- Communication   –   furthering two-way communication.

Task Oriented

- Organisation and Control   –   effectively arranging and monitoring the work of individuals and teams.

- Providing resources   –   supporting and giving the means for people to do good work.

- Decision making   –   analysing problems and identifying solutions.

- Planning   –   developing work plans and objectives.

- Delegation   –   achieving through others but retaining personal accountability.

Remember that your job as a Manager is to achieve the task through other people. Both these aspects of management need to be addressed so don't neglect the task in favour of managing your people or vice versa. Strive to be a Balanced Manager.

You will need to get involved in each of these ten aspects of management but the emphasis will vary according to the situation you are managing. This means that:

- You need to understand what is involved and to be competent in each activity. Don't concentrate on those which you find easier and ignore the others. All the components of managment must be applied if you are to be effective.

- You need to determine whether the situation or individuals that you are managing require special emphasis on one or more of the activities.

It is useful to compare your own views with those of your boss and your people on how you are doing as a Manager. Try to get a clear picture of those activities where you are perceived to be effective and those where improvement is required.

Manage efficiently

The secret is to get **yourself** organised. If you don't do this, you will find that you are frantically busy but achieving little. Being disorganised has a number of unhealthy side effects on your life, like not having time for anything but work. Chaos is also contagious and disorganisation is likely to spread to others. Your lack of personal organisation will put an enormous strain on yourself, your family and all the people who work with you. It is in everyone's interest to make sure that you are well organised.

You have to work at organising yourself effectively. There are lots of different means to the same end and a whole series of textbooks and courses exist to help you. A useful shortcut can be to ask someone who you know is well organised about their systems and approach. There is no need to re-invent the wheel.

Ultimately, you must develop the approach which is right for you, but here are some of the fundamentals of organising yourself well:

Manage time

Discipline yourself and make good use of your time to get things done. That means doing the things you planned on doing, when you planned on doing them and for no longer than you planned. There are two essentials – planning your time and not wasting your time. Here are some key points:

- Make a 'To Do' list. Use an Action Pad and keep a current list of **everything** you have to do.

- Prioritise what you have to do. Take account of urgency and importance.

- Use your diary to schedule when to do each task and how long to spend on it. Try to stick to your schedule.

Manage Paper

- Don't spend all your time on reactive day-to-day tasks. Make time for tasks which you must do to achieve your objectives.

- Make arrangements so that you're not interrupted when you want time to yourself or need to get something done.

- Do it now. Get on with things that can be done today. Don't put things off – it leads to inefficiency.

- Motivate yourself to tackle the jobs that you find hard or unpleasant. You'll get a sense of achievement when you've done them.

- Make rather than waste time when using the telephone.

- From time to time, analyse how you spend your time at work. Is it effective?

- As a Manager, you consume other people's time. Don't waste it!

Manage paper

Paperwork will get on top of you if you don't get on top of it. (The state of your desk will give an indication of whether or not you're winning.) Managing paper efficiently involves both reading and writing. Again, a few tips:

- Don't write unnecessarily. Writing creates you work and reading takes others' time.

- Use memos primarily to pass on information. It's usually easier to deal with contentious matters by discussion.

- When you write, get it right. Written work gives an impression of you – watch out for accuracy, spelling and errors.

- Keep your distribution and copies lists to the minimum and take yourself off unnecessary distribution lists.

- Keep a chronological file of all your own correspondence This reduces the number of subject files you have to keep and makes things easier to find.

- Keep filing to a minimum. Use central or shared files wherever possible and purge historic files ruthlessly.

- Quickly sort your post into Urgent Action, Non-Urgent Action and Reading. Go through it in that order and deal with each item as you read it if possible. (Remember – Try to Process Paper Only Once.)

Manage to remember

As a Manager, you'll have a lot on your mind. It's useful to have a system to jog your memory:

- Write down the things you have to do as they crop up. Then build them into your 'To Do' list.

- Take notes. It aids understanding and recall.

- Use a bring forward file and your diary to plan the future.

- Diarise the key dates affecting your people – appraisal, long-service anniversary and so on.

- Use a loose-leaf file or labelled plastic folder for building up agendas, items for progress meetings, monthly reports and so on.

- Keep an on-going list of things to discuss with other people. Raise three or four points together – it's more efficient.

- Always return telephone calls. Discipline yourself to do this within twenty-four hours.

Manage your secretary

If you do have secretarial support (which is not possible for everyone), use this to the best advantage. Make it a partnership and let your secretary help you manage yourself. You need to:

- Make sure your secretary understands how you organise yourself (and helps you to improve if necessary).

- Involve your secretary in diary planning and scheduling. A regular weekly meeting to do this is useful.

- Agree the basis on which you are interruptable.

- Always communicate where you are and how you can be contacted.

- Utilise your secretary as much as possible and delegate where you can. This includes correspondence, keeping records, co-ordinating holidays, arranging meetings and so on. Most secretaries can and want to do more.

- Train your secretary to remind you about things. This can be a useful backstop.

- Use, don't abuse your secretarial support. There might be times when it could be more efficient if you made the tea!

Delegate

Delegation is a key management activity which allows you to achieve through others and free yourself to spend time on priorities. Delegation is not abdication. It means giving people who report to you the responsibility and authority to achieve something on your behalf whilst you retain account-ability – i.e. you carry the can. Through delegation, you can manage yourself better, achieve results through others and develop your people at the same time. However, it is impor-tant to delegate properly as this maximises the benefits and minimises the risks.

Plan what to delegate

- First ask yourself what you can delegate and what benefits there would be in somebody else doing parts of your job.

- You might need to accept that initially the task might take longer and be to a lesser quality than you could achieve yourself.

- Remember that delegation is not 'dumping' – an opportunity to off-load all the boring or difficult tasks.

Delegate Properly

- Try to select whole tasks that will provide the person with some 'stretch' and a sense of achievement when complete.

- Assess the level of risk on vital tasks before delegating them. Keep direct responsibility for things that you just can't afford to delegate (which includes your role as the Manager).

- Give clear direction. Don't delegate tasks which are vague and will require your people to spend time and effort on clarification.

Decide to whom to delegate

- Check out the capacity and the willingness of individuals to handle the work.

- Delegate to those who are competent or are likely to be capable of achieving the task with coaching/training.

- Delegation is a development opportunity. Try to provide a new learning experience for the individual.

- Always encourage delegation as far down your organisation as possible. People will feel committed and motivated that you trust them to achieve (and will invariably rise to the challenge).

Delegate properly

Before delegating, you should:

- Ensure that the individual understands the reason for delegation, including the levels of responsibility and authority that you have given and what support can be expected.

- Give precise instructions on what you want to be achieved (what, by when and to what standards) but give discretion on how this is to be done.

- Ensure that arrangements for reporting progress and seeking help are clearly understood.

- Let other people who are likely to be affected know what is happening.

During delegation you should:

- Use regular checks and a series of progress meetings to monitor progress.
- Build confidence. Be available for advice but don't 'help' by double checking, changing every decision and so on.
- Give constructive feedback and praise on an on-going basis but don't breathe down the person's neck. Give some elbow room and make allowance for mistakes.

On completion of the task:

- Evaluate performance and give feedback on the learning points.
- Always thank the individual for helping (and give recognition when appropriate).
- Re-define the job description if there are any permanent changes to job content.

Checklist 1

Managing Yourself

Understand Yourself

- Evaluate yourself
- Seek feedback from others

Manage Effectively

- Be clear about what you are expected to achieve
- Get the right balance between doing and managing
- Get the right emphasis between your management activities

Manage Efficiently

- Manage time
- Manage paper
- Manage to remember
- Manage your secretary

Delegate

- Plan what to delegate
- Decide to whom to delegate
- Delegate properly

2 MANAGING OTHERS

The guiding principle here is Positive Management. Your aim must be to achieve results by managing people well, providing them with the best leadership possible. Managing other people to these standards is a tough challenge, so what are the essentials of getting it right? What should you be doing to make sure that you're a Positive Manager?

Of course, there are no magic answers but the following section is a reminder of some of the tried and tested Do's and Don'ts of managing other people. For convenience, these are grouped under three headings:

- Lead by Example
- Build Working Relationships
- Manage for Results.

Just before this, here are a couple of tips which you might find helpful when managing people. Firstly, think about Positive Managers whom you know and analyse why they are effective. What can you learn and apply from them? Secondly, always try to put yourself in the position of the people you're managing. Then you will manage others as you would like to be managed yourself.

Lead by example

Leaders set an example to their people in everything they do. Don't underestimate your standing. Your people will be influenced by your personal attitude, behaviour and performance. You always need to set a good example for others to follow. Unless you do this, you won't get their full commitment and support and achievement will suffer. The essentials here are:

Work hard to high standards

If you want your people to work hard, work hard yourself. Otherwise, they will begin to ask themselves why they should bother. Also, by producing high quality work yourself, you set the standards for your people and they will then know what is expected.

Be positive

If you show enthusiasm and energy, this will be infectious. People will share your commitment and be motivated to achieve.

How you project yourself is a vital factor in determining the morale of your team. You need to manage your own morale and motivation. Be positive whenever you can. People would prefer to be managed by someone who is cheerful and optimistic rather than a person who moans and groans. Remember to share the highs and hide the lows. If things aren't going well, don't mislead people but avoid spreading gloom and despondency or predicting the worst.

Be corporate

That doesn't mean blind obedience or having to accept that everything's perfect when it's not. Being corporate means not 'knocking' the Company or other Managers and not publicly voicing any disagreement that you may have on corporate policy or decisions. 'Cabinet responsibility' is part of being a Manager. If you can't positively support or you have a concern, express your views up the organisation rather than sharing them with your people.

Help out

Leading from the front sometimes means rolling up your sleeves. Help out if circumstances demand it – your people will appreciate it, even if you can't do the job as well as them! It also shows that you are prepared to tackle what you usually ask other people to do.

Don't panic

Don't get emotionally involved with tasks but try to keep your head when all about you are losing theirs. If you keep calm in a crisis, your example will keep others cool and enable you to manage things more effectively.

Don't compromise yourself

Never weaken your position as a result of your behaviour. As a Manager, you need to be seen as mature and responsible, able to conduct yourself properly in every situation. That doesn't mean being starchy and not joining in the fun – but don't go over the top.

Be careful not to put yourself in a position where you can't raise issues with your people because of your own behaviour. For example, it's very difficult to manage poor timekeeping by others if you can be criticised yourself for this.

Don't let it get you down!

Life as a Manager should be enjoyable (even if things don't go smoothly all the time). Stick at it and be tenacious but try to keep things in perspective. Don't go about as if you're carrying the world on your shoulders. Keep your sense of fun and humour and don't take criticism too personally.

Build working relationships

To achieve through others, you need to build effective working relationships through mutual trust and respect. When a good working relationship has been developed, people will give of their best, achieve results and gain personal satisfaction.

Earn trust and respect

You have to earn trust and respect as a Manager – it doesn't come automatically with the title. As a Manager, it is essential that you are trusted and respected and this is more important than popularity or being liked.

Don't Let It Get You Down!

So what do you need to do to earn trust and respect from your people?

Be yourself

Manage in a style which comes naturally to you. By all means try to project your best self – but don't try to be something you're not. People will see through you.

Be human

You don't have to be superhuman to be a Manager. It often strengthens others' respect for you if you admit that you don't know something. You're not expected to know it all.

It is also better to ask for help than to fail for want of it. We all need assistance at some time, so there's no need to feel inadequate. It's often useful and beneficial to share your problems with other Managers or your boss. No-one has the monopoly of all the good ideas and right answers, and inputs from others can often lead to superior solutions.

Finally, don't pretend that you are infallible. Admit your mistakes rather than looking for excuses or someone to blame. Instead, get on with putting them right and avoiding a repetition.

Be consistent

Try to behave consistently so that your people know how to 'read' you. When people know and understand you, they are more likely to trust you, be open and say what they think. When your reactions are unpredictable, they will be anxious and clam up. The general rule here should be 'No Surprises' – there are plenty of other areas to demonstrate your creativity as a Manager!

Be fair

Always ensure that your people get a fair deal. A good general rule is always to treat other people as you would like to be treated yourself. Being fair also includes:

- Not demanding too much or caring too little
- Not having favourites or showing favouritism
- Being aware of any personal prejudices or bias
- Giving the benefit of the doubt
- Not jumping to conclusions before investigating all the facts
- Supporting people rather than trying to catch them out
- Thinking through the likely impact of your decisions and judgements
- Checking sensitive judgements and decisions with other people before acting
- Checking for precedents and ensuring consistency
- Making sure that any unfairness or injustice is put right as soon as possible.

Be trustworthy

It is vital that your people feel relaxed about confiding in you and know that you are discreet. As their Manager, you must show integrity to be credible. The trust that this produces is vital to your effectiveness as a Manager. Remember that trust can be quickly lost and is difficult to re-establish, so:

- Be sincere. Do and mean what you say
- Don't mislead or 'con' people. (Remember that this can still happen if you don't tell the whole truth)
- Say what you think (but do think before you say it)
- Be dependable and reliable
- Keep your promises and never promise what you can't deliver
- Be discreet. Respect confidences and confidentiality
- Avoid expedient, short-term decisions.

Show trust and respect

If you are to lead people effectively and achieve results through their efforts, you must put your trust in them and value their contribution. To build a working relationship with the people in your team you should:

Know your people

Everyone is different. Avoid 'labelling' people and manage them as individuals.

Develop a genuine interest in each person. Stop to chat when you can and ask how things are. It's also a useful opportunity for them to get to know you. There's no need to get involved or probe into people's private lives, but you do need to know and understand about the people who work for you to build up an effective relationship. Make time available for your people – it is well worthwhile.

Be caring and considerate

As a Manager, you have a responsibility to look after your people in the widest sense. You need to have genuine concern and interest in them. They must be able to rely on you to protect and represent their interests and try hard to help with their problems. This sometimes means that you have to take the initiative rather than wait to be asked or prompted.

It may not be possible to please everyone or accommodate their wishes, but there is no excuse for an issue developing into a grievance because of neglect on your part. You must always try to do right by people but, if what they want or need is just not possible or appropriate, make sure that they know that is the case and understand the reason why.

Being considerate means treating people in the right way. It involves finding time for them and listening. Put yourself in the other person's shoes and consider their feelings. Be pleas-

Be Caring and Considerate

ant and deal sensitively with people. Treat them as equals, showing the same respect and courtesy that you would expect yourself. Try to find ways of helping people maintain their sense of dignity and self esteem. Avoid making them feel humiliated or hurt. Think twice before you lose your temper or say something that you may regret later.

Encourage involvement

Never underestimate the interest that people have in what is going on around them. Involve people on issues where they have knowledge, experience and can make a contribution. Some of the best information, views and ideas will come from the people who work with the detail of the area that you are managing. Don't stifle their creativity or block ideas even if some are not presented in a polished, thought-through way. You are still responsible for final decisions, but involving people can generate better solutions and shows that you value their input. It also brings them satisfaction and greater commitment to the end result.

Do remember that if you ask for ideas, you need to take them seriously. Use them wherever possible or be careful to explain why not. If you don't do this, you won't get any more next time. Thank people for their input even if you don't use it.

Consult and explain

Wherever possible advise your people in advance of things which affect them. Apart from being polite, it makes sense to prepare people for change and give them time to get used to the idea. Ask for suggestions on how things can be done better and try to build in their ideas.

Take time to explain the background to issues in which people are directly involved or have an interest. This is always appreciated, and understanding the wider context often helps people to improve their performance and think for themselves.

Help to achieve

Give your people help and encouragement. Show them that you want them to succeed and do everything you can to make that happen. Interest and encouragement from you can be very motivational. Use your influence to help them get things done and add value by constructive thoughts, suggestions and ideas. Avoid damaging people by destructive criticism or disparaging remarks. Don't make changes to other people's work unnecessarily. Nit-picking frustrates people.

Don't take the credit for achievements that are not yours. Give the kudos to your people and take pride in the success of your team. Help people to avoid making mistakes, although they will still occur from time to time where people are learning or using their initiative. Rather than looking to allocate blame (which only generates excuses) make sure that individuals learn from mistakes. Your aim should be to prevent repetition not administer retribution, but don't be so tolerant if the same mistake is made again.

Encourage openness

Make sure that your people know that you want them to be open and give their views on how things are going and how they are being managed. Make it clear that you need to know both the good and the bad news in order to be able to manage effectively.

It's vital that people know that there will be no recrimination for speaking openly but do establish a rule that all criticism needs to be constructive. This means that when people raise a problem they should also try to suggest a solution.

Be trusting

As management is about getting things done through people, you have to put your trust in others. If people are capable, let them get on with things and give them freedom to operate. Wherever possible, encourage others to think for themselves and be creative.

Over-control and over-checking will be seen as lack of trust and will reduce the extent to which people will use their initiative.

Try to work on the basis of maximum trust and the fewest rules possible. If people are treated responsibly, they will normally respond accordingly, and not abuse your faith in them. Always work on the basis of trusting a person until there is a reason not to.

Manage by consent

Try to get the support of your people for what you want to do. Wherever possible:

- Ask rather than tell

- Only instruct people and exert your authority to get things done if you absolutely have to

- Explain the reasons for things to people first and listen to what they have to say

- Take account of their views if you can and give reasons if you can't.

By seeking to manage by consent, you will gain the commitment of people to achieving what needs to be done. Convincing people that what you want to do is right reinforces rather than undermines your position as a Manager. There may be situations where you do have to act without their agreement, but still explain why.

Manage for results

Results are the 'bottom line' of being a Manager. You need to ensure that your team delivers what is required on time, to the right quality and cost (and feels well managed at the same time). Don't be afraid to take risks but also don't take short-cuts without being aware of the implications. To manage for results, you need to:

Set high standards

Recruit only high calibre people. Select only those who you know are going to perform well and don't compromise on recruitment standards. If in doubt, don't appoint or you will have to manage sub-standard performance as a consequence in future.

Always run a tight ship. Set performance standards that are demanding but achievable so that people feel stretched and can take pride in what they do. Make sure that everyone is doing necessary work and is kept busy. Morale and performance levels fall when people don't have enough to do. On the other hand, make sure that you don't demand too much.

Don't be complacent – keep trying to improve your own and your people's performance and efficiency.

Give clear direction

Make sure that everyone is clear on what needs to be achieved. Provide your people with objectives, including timescales and the standards required. Set priorities and keep them under review. Don't tackle too much or too many things at once.

Make sound decisions

To manage for results, you need to decide what to do and go for it. That calls for good judgement and timing to make the right decisions and strong resolve to stick with them.

When a decision needs to be made, avoid acting on impulse and shooting from the hip. Also beware of the other extreme, dithering and never actually making up your mind. Be methodical – gather all the data you require and then consider the pros and cons. Don't be rushed – it's usually better to mull things over a little longer and get the decision right first time.

If things change subsequently, review your decisions and be flexible enough to change them if you have to. However, make sure that there are good reasons for this and that you are not just bowing to pressure from others. You may still be right.

Face up to issues

Don't be a Good News Manager. If you always ignore problems and issues and only tell people what they want to hear, you are not facing up to your responsibilities. Problems will usually not go away, and by not tackling things that you know are wrong, you compound the difficulties. If you ignore substandard performance or behaviour, you are condoning it. You will be seen as weak and ineffective and standards will drop overall. Your people will certainly not thank you for letting things slide. No matter how unpalatable or sensitive the issues, don't put off the appropriate action. Deal with it promptly, firmly and fairly, or results will suffer.

You need to be seen to be accountable. That means that there are times when you've got to stand up and be counted. If your boss wants to know why your area is not performing, don't put the blame on your people when it is your fault. If you can't deliver what your people want, don't put the blame on senior management, the job evaluation system or anything else. When results aren't forthcoming, accept your responsibility and 'take the heat'. Don't be a Transparent Manager.

Keep control

To do this, you need to know what's happening in your area. Keep in touch with what is going on. Have regular checkpoints and progress meetings with your people. It's also useful to check things out yourself from time to time. By talking to your people who don't report directly to you, you can very often get a good feel for what's happening on the ground. It's best to let your management hierarchy know that you're going to do this and explain the reasons why – otherwise they may feel threatened.

Always be accessible and encourage your people to keep you posted on likely problems. If you know about things at the outset, major crises can be averted and issues can be nipped in the bud.

Recognise achievement

Give feedback and recognise good results. This applies to individuals and the team. It will add to the satisfaction that your people get for a job well done and will motivate them to achieve again.

Always thank your people for their efforts. Be sincere and don't de-value recognition by overdoing it or praising insignificant achievements.

Recognise Achievement

Managing Others

Lead by Example

- Work hard to high standards
- Be positive
- Be corporate
- Help out
- Don't panic
- Don't compromise yourself
- Don't let it get you down

Build Working Relationships

- Earn Trust and Respect
- Be yourself
- Be human
- Be consistent
- Be fair
- Be trustworthy
- Show Trust and Respect
- Know your people
- Be caring and considerate
- Encourage involvement
- Consult and explain
- Help to achieve
- Encourage openness
- Be trusting
- Manage by consent

Manage for Results

- Set high standards
- Give clear direction
- Make sound decisions
- Face up to issues
- Keep control
- Recognise achievement

3 MANAGING YOUR BOSS

Working effectively with your own Manager is as important as managing yourself and your people well. Whilst not forgetting who is boss, your aim should be to develop a working partnership. As you are both working to the same goals and have a shared interest in success, this is the ideal relationship. You should be aware that partnership may not suit everyone's style but there are always benefits in seeking to manage the relationship positively, so try to:

Develop understanding

Get to know how your Manager operates. Think through how to work most effectively with that individual's approach, pace and style. Usually, the best way to improve your relationship is to see what you can do, not what you can get your Manager to do. Help carry the load, don't add to it by delegating all the 'nasties' upwards.

Try to see things from your Manager's position to get a clearer picture of the pressures and constraints which apply at that level. By understanding those problems you will be in a better position to assist.

Also ensure that your Manager is able to see things from your point of view. Find ways to give a first-hand understanding of the realities of your situation and how you operate.

Keep informed

Keep each other up-to-date with what is going on and work on the basis of 'No Surprises'. Make sure that your Manager is never 'caught out' by not knowing about things that you should have communicated. Be open and frank, but try not to

Keep Informed

shock. Break bad news without over-dramatising the situation.

Use your Manager as a sounding-board on ideas and what you are planning to do. This gives early warning and usually makes for a better result. Identify issues which are developing and flag up such situations early, highlighting any danger signals.

Present solutions not problems

Wherever possible, hold off raising a problem until you have had a chance to review potential solutions. Put forward those possible solutions at the same time as you raise the problem. Apart from taking some of the load off your Manager, it might also avoid an imposed solution that you might find difficult to live with.

Show initiative

Use your initiative, but don't overstep the mark or take on too much too soon. Expand your influence gradually and build up your Manager's confidence in you. Take one step at a time and show that you can take on some of the load. Your aim should then be to become an experienced and able deputy.

Be businesslike

Get to know how your Manager likes things done and fit in with those preferences.

Make your Manager's job easier by doing as much groundwork as possible yourself. Rather than passing across lots of reading and just asking for a decision, briefly summarise the key points at issue, present arguments for and against particular courses of action, and put forward your views and recommendations wherever appropriate.

Before raising a topic, make sure that you have done your homework and are well prepared. (That includes thinking through your Manager's likely reaction to what you are raising.) Also be sure to choose the right moment. Avoid raising something when there is not time to deal with it properly or the person is not going to be receptive.

Give support

Both you and your Manager are ideally situated to know the weaker points in each other's performance and to improve your joint performance as a result. There may be areas where your Manager does not have your skills and strengths (and vice versa). Complement each other's performance by asking for and offering support. Never be afraid to ask for help. It is always better to do this rather than run the risk of crisis or failure.

Try to reach an agreement that you both have the responsibility to comment on how the other's performance can be improved. Not every Manager will be open to the idea, but mutual feedback can be valuable. Be open with your Manager by raising any concerns directly. If you can, get your message across without rubbing in faults and mistakes and always avoid embarrassing or ridiculing. Finally, do your best to keep each other 'out of jail' by watching for likely own goals and mistakes.

Disagree positively

There will be times when you disagree with your Manager, but don't be afraid to challenge. Express your views, but try not to be negative or emotional. Seek explanations and probe the reasons for decisions. Back up your arguments with facts and evidence. Don't just disagree – offer solutions and alternatives. Argue for what you believe is right as objectively as you can. However, if you are overruled at the end of the day, put personal views aside and manage the situation positively. Be loyal and don't complain to others.

Overall, if you follow this supportive and open approach, you are likely to be given more autonomy and increased responsibility in return. Both you and your Manager stand to gain from this sort of teamwork.

Checklist 3

Managing Your Boss

- Develop understanding
- Keep informed
- Present solutions not problems
- Show initiative
- Be businesslike
- Give support
- Disagree positively

4 MANAGING PERFORMANCE

Management is all about achieving results through others, so managing the performance of your people is a central focus for your efforts.

Essentially you need to:

- Ensure that everyone is clear about what to do and the standards required
- Keep yourself informed on how things are going
- Provide the necessary help and support to achieve what is required
- Seek to improve individual performance at all times.

All this involves spending a few hours each week on setting objectives and reviewing progress. Managing the performance of individuals may be summarised as:

- Planning performance
- Tracking performance
- Improving performance.

By following this approach, and **regularly** investing time in managing performance, everyone will be more effective.

Plan performance

Managing performance begins with planning. The aim of planning is to start performance off in the right direction. It is a process of objective setting by which you ensure that each individual who reports to you understands what results and standards are to be achieved. This is best summarised in writing as a Performance Plan and the steps in producing this are listed below:

Identify goals

Think through carefully what you want the individual to achieve overall. This needs to be consistent with the wider strategy and priorities established for your area by your boss.

Individual goals will vary in range and scope. Some will cover the daily responsibilities of the job and other duties which keep the work flowing properly at acceptable levels of quality. Others will relate to areas where specific improvements need to be made or new approaches developed. Determine the right balance between maintenance, improvement and development when you identify goals for individuals. When the person is also a Manager, it is important to get the right balance between managing people and achieving the task. Here the goals for the individual should take into account what needs to be achieved in people management terms as well.

Finally, as you are identifying goals for the next twelve months or so, you need to prioritise what has to be achieved. This might be difficult but try to determine what is most important and where time and resource needs to be concentrated. If possible, spread the timing of high priorities over the period to reduce the risk of overload.

Set objectives

Having identified what is to be achieved, break this down into precise, workable steps as objectives for the individual. Make sure that the objectives you set are:

- **Specific**

  An objective should state a result not an activity and be written in clear, simple language.

- **Attainable**

  The objective itself must be reasonable and the individual must have the necessary skill, knowledge and ability or be able to acquire it quickly. However, there also needs to be

Set Objectives

some challenge and 'stretch'. This should vary depending upon the capacity and capability of the person, as objectives which are either too hard or too easy will demotivate.

- **Measurable**

  Wherever possible, quantify the objective. This includes setting down the standards required. When objectives are measurable, it is easier to agree subsequently on what has been achieved.

- **Timebound**

  Include target dates. Specify when the results must be achieved and don't leave an objective open-ended.

What does all this mean in practice? The aim is a comprehensive working document containing the main results required. Avoid long lists and try to distil the essentials. Always ensure that objectives are clear-cut rather than woolly statements of intent. For example, instead of 'Manage Performance Effectively', a better statement of objectives would be 'Ensure that every individual has a Performance Plan and a schedule of Progress Meetings. Complete all outstanding Performance Appraisals by year-end'.

Agree objectives

It is important to discuss and jointly agree objectives. This ensures understanding of what is required and 'contracting' in this way increases commitment. The whole process of discussion up-front ensures that the objectives are reasonable and that priorities are clear and understood. Agreement now avoids disagreement later – but if you can't agree, the final say-so is yours.

With an experienced person, it is sometimes useful to ask the individual to set their own objectives which you can then agree. 'Bottom-up' objective setting like this can aid individual development.

Write a performance plan

Objectives need to be written up into a Performance Plan for each individual. This is a statement of what has to be done and the standards to be achieved. As a statement of results to be achieved, a Performance Plan is likely to be different from a job description, which is more a broad statement of on-going duties.

Performance Plans can range from a formal set of objectives through to Terms of Reference for a specific piece of work or just an *ad hoc* note of what is to be achieved. Whatever the format, the important thing is to document objectives in writing as simply as possible. Both you and the individual then need to keep a copy for ready reference.

Update the performance plan

The Performance Plan is dynamic and will need to be reviewed and amended as things change. Target dates and standards should be altered if these prove impossible or too easy to meet. Always watch for unrealistic targets or insufficient challenge. Also, as objectives are achieved, new results required should be added. You must manage the plan and, at any point in time, the individual should have a very clear idea of what the priorities and objectives are.

Track performance

Having agreed a Performance Plan, it is vital that you monitor and review performance against this on a continuing basis to ensure that the individual is 'on track'.

The process of tracking performance is essential to ensure that your people achieve what is required. Setting objectives and just hoping that they will be achieved is not managing performance and does not work. You need to establish proper information systems to keep yourself informed and run a series of progress meetings to review how things are going, adjust direction and priorities as necessary and feedback on performance. Make sure that you:

Stay informed

You need an effective information system to be able to monitor how things are going 'at a glance'. Obtain regular reports on key measures of performance (for example, volumes, quality, costs and so on) from each area for which you are responsible. Keep the level of effort to produce this down to a minimum. Wherever possible, use the information which your people already have to help them manage or do their job.

Maintain an efficient weekly copies system so that you are in the picture on everything that is going on. Also make sure that your people know that you want to be kept informed and are available for help if things are not going smoothly or if they want advice or guidance.

Review progress

Use one-to-one progress meetings to check things out and improve performance.

- **Establish a schedule**

  The frequency with which you hold progress meetings will depend upon your particular situation but always have a plan for a regular series of meetings over the review period. Stick to the pattern and supplement this with *ad hoc* meetings as necessary. Some progress meetings may be short updates whilst others may be wide-ranging, in-depth sessions which tie into the monthly/annual reporting process.

- **Prepare for progress meetings**

  Preparation will save time and increase effectiveness. Keep a progress file and gather items for your next progress meeting as you go along. Jot down topics as they occur to you and make a list of what you want to discuss at the meeting. Encourage the other person to prepare for progress meetings in just the same way.

- **Get the most out of progress meetings**

  The main aim of the meeting is to ensure that the performance is on track against the objectives and priorities set down in the Performance Plan. Check back against this and if things have changed, modify the Plan accordingly.

  Use the meeting to get a close picture of what is going on and identify the main problems and vulnerabilities. Discuss how these can be overcome and agree what needs to be done to improve performance.

  Take the opportunity to use some progress meetings as 'mini-appraisals'. Feedback on specific aspects of individual and team performance and then nothing will come as a surprise at the main Appraisal. Don't duck issues and leave things unsaid. Invite comment and ensure two-way communication.

  Finally, ensure that action points are clearly communicated. Without being too bureaucratic, issue minutes or a record of the main action points arising for future reference and keep a note on any performance feedback that has been given. This can save you quite a lot of time when preparing for the Performance Appraisal.

Improve performance

As a Manager, your role is to help your people achieve results and give of their best. Your approach towards their performance should be directed at improvement and you should always seek to:

Encourage

Show interest in what and how your people are doing and let

Get the Most Out of Progress Meetings

them know that you want and expect them to do well. If you make it clear that you have high (but not unreasonable) standards and expectations, people will strive to meet them and respond positively to your confidence in them.

Always look for the positives in performance. It's so easy to spend time on problems and concerns, and you do need to do this. However, keep a sense of balance and when a task has been done well, praise performance. This lets people know that they are achieving and that you appreciate their efforts, and it encourages them to achieve in the future. Remember to praise people immediately, tell them what they did right and let them know that you were pleased about it. Don't underestimate the impact this has on people and their performance.

In the same way, don't overlook mistakes or poor performance. Raise your concerns with people at the time. Let them know what they did wrong. Be constructive and don't rub it in. Make it clear that your aim is to help the individual improve and avoid a repetition.

Help and support

You need to provide all your people with appropriate support and direction. This will vary between individuals and it really does mean different strokes for different folks. Some individuals you will be able to leave alone and be confident that results will be excellent. Others you will need to help and direct in varying amounts along the way. Think through what support each individual needs in any situation in order to perform well. The amount of support that you need to give will depend upon the competence and confidence of the person undertaking the task. In very simple terms, this can be seen at three levels:

- You need to **direct** people who are inexperienced or lack the right level of ability to achieve the job. This means telling them what to do, how to do it, where and when to do it and then closely supervising their performance.

- You need to coach and **support** people who are becoming competent but are not yet confident. They may not require too much direction but do need your involvement in problem solving and decision making and for you to recognise and praise their progress. Make sure that you are available for help or guidance as required.

- You can **delegate** to people who are able and willing to achieve results by themselves without supervision or support.

In essence, you need to do what the people you supervise can't do for themselves yet. As individuals develop competence and confidence, you can provide less supervision and support and allow them to manage themselves.

Give feedback

It is essential to let people know how they are doing. Ongoing feedback on performance helps the person know where they stand and what, if anything, they should be doing differently. It keeps people on track, provides recognition and assists learning and development.

Pick things up as they happen or at the next progress meeting – don't duck giving feedback or put it off until appraisal time. That leads to resentment and nasty surprises – "You didn't say anything about that at the time". People are more likely to improve if you give them feedback immediately rather than long after the event.

Giving performance feedback in a constructive way requires skill, understanding and respect for others. Always keep the impact on the individual in mind and remember to:

- Be objective. Base feedback on facts not inference or judgements which cannot be substantiated. Give examples.

- Be balanced. There is usually room for some improvement in good performance and some good points in overall poor performance.

- Concentrate on **behaviour** not personality. It is easier to counsel someone about what to do differently rather than about what sort of person they are.

- Structure feedback for the benefit of the receiver, not just to let off steam yourself.

By following these rules, you are likely to have a positive effect on performance rather than provoke a negative, emotional reaction.

Appraise performance

The formal Performance Appraisal pulls together all aspects of an individual's performance over a period. This is straightforward if you have reviewed performance on an on-going basis and the Appraisal should then contain no surprises for you or the individual. If you have not done the groundwork, the more difficult Performance Appraisal becomes and the longer it takes. Your aim at Performance Appraisal should be to strengthen overall performance by discussing:

- What was achieved against the objectives set for the period

- Your overall view of performance, including strengths and weaknesses

- What needs to be done to improve performance and the help and support you will give

- Direction and objectives for the period ahead

- What the individual wants to do in future.

In addition, the Performance Appraisal is a good opportunity to get feedback on wider issues and on your own performance. Every individual is entitled to a thorough and objective Appraisal.

Tackle Poor Performance Positively

Whatever method you use, appraisals should be done to the following standards.

- Appraisal should normally take place annually except for transfers, new starters or when there is a change of boss or responsibility when six months may be more appropriate.

- Appraisal does not coincide with Salary Reviews to keep the emphasis on performance rather than reward.

- You give adequate notice of Appraisal and you both prepare beforehand.

- All aspects are discussed face-to-face and are recorded.

- The individual and your boss check and sign off the Appraisal.

Finally, don't forget that no matter how long someone has been in a job, performance can always be improved. There is still a need for Appraisal, even if this is only a short discussion.

Tackle poor performance positively

At some time, you are likely to be faced with a person who is unable or unwilling to perform satisfactorily. Tackle the problem with a view to improving performance and only use punitive measures like demotion, discipline and termination as a last resort when other means won't work.

Rather than just writing off the individual adopt a positive approach:

- Keep a record and analyse the poor performance carefully. Exactly what behaviour is giving you a problem? Do other Managers see the level of performance in the same way? Do you have enough objective evidence to justify the concern?

- Try to identify the main cause of poor performance (remembering that there may be several). Your approach to lack of ability or knowledge could well be different from problems of motivation. Are you part of the performance problem? Managers can cause performance to deteriorate by giving unchallenging tasks, not giving feedback or providing development, generating uncertainty and so on.

- Tackle poor performance early. Don't tolerate poor performance because it is too much trouble to deal with or in the hope that it might get better by itself. The longer you leave it the worse things will get, others will be affected and your own credibility will suffer.

- Talk the problem and your plan through with your boss beforehand as two heads are always better than one.

- Communicate your concerns to the individual face-to-face and try to help through a problem-solving approach. Agree where performance has been unsatisfactory and what needs to change. Identify the standard required and develop an action plan to help achieve this. Set a date to follow-up and review progress.

- Consider whether changing the content of the job or a complete change of job would help improve performance (especially if the main cause of difficulty is level of ability). However, don't do this just to pass the problem on to somebody else.

- Encourage improved performance with positive feedback.

Checklist 4

Managing Performance

Plan Performance

- Identify goals
- Set and agree objectives
- Write a Performance Plan
- Update the Performance Plan

Track Performance

- Stay informed
- Review progress

Improve Performance

- Encourage
- Help and support
- Give feedback
- Appraise performance
- Tackle poor performance positively

5 MANAGING DISCIPLINE AND GRIEVANCES

First and foremost, be positive. Trust people to act respon-sibly, treat everyone fairly and well, and tackle issues and concerns early. Performance and motivation will then be good and the incidence of formal discipline and complaints will be minimal. However, no matter how well you manage, disciplinary or grievance situations may still crop up occasionally and you need to know how to approach them.

Discipline fairly

Discipline can range from an informal warning to dismissal. Whatever the circumstances, the guiding principles for hand-ling discipline are the same:

- Prevention is better than cure! Wherever possible, try to avoid the need for any discipline by anticipating and guiding the actions of the individual.

- The purpose of discipline is to identify and help correct lapses from high standards of conduct and work, not to punish or hurt the individual.

- It's always worth discussing and mulling things over with somebody else (usually your boss) rather than taking action on your own.

- Always tackle situations requiring discipline firmly. Don't duck the issue (however unpleasant) or other people will relax their own standards and blame you for letting others 'get away with it'.

- Your 'jurisdiction' over people's private lives only extends to actions which impact on work.

- Justice not only has to be seen but also felt to be done. You need to be both consistent and fair rather than be seen as a 'Macho' Manager. The ultimate test of equity is that the employee feels fairly treated and agrees with the actions taken.

- Dismissal is always the last resort.

Every disciplinary case is different in detail and needs individual and sensitive handling. However, the following general approach may help:

Identify the standards required

You need to make clear the standards of conduct and work performance that are required. It is up to you to ensure that every individual understands what is expected (and what is not!) from the outset. If at any time you decide that it is necessary to tighten up standards which have become lax or are not generally observed, it is important to give ample warning and explanation as to why. Do not suddenly take action and 'drop' on people without warning.

Know and follow the disciplinary procedure

Establish a disciplinary procedure to provide a fair and consistent method of dealing with failure to meet your standards. You should consider incorporating the Code of Practice established by the Advisory, Conciliation and Arbitration Service (ACAS) into your own procedure. Ensure that your people know and understand what this is. The informal warning is probably the most important step in the whole disciplinary process, with a very good chance of getting the individual concerned to conform and perform correctly. However, if the necessary improvement is not made, then you need to follow up with a first written warning and, if necessary, go through the procedure until it is finally exhausted. Of course, more serious forms of misconduct may justify an immediate written warning or dismissal.

Act promptly

You need to pick up unacceptable behaviour and performance at the time it occurs. Unless you take prompt, firm action, you are condoning lower standards and encouraging a drift into bad habits. However, acting promptly does not mean impetuously. Allow yourself the time necessary to plan and investigate beforehand and let the individual know that you will be raising the matter if this results in delay.

Investigate and consult beforehand

It is important to be as well informed as possible before raising the issue with the individual. This does not mean pre-judging the outcome, but you do need to be able to state the complaint with some precision and present supporting evidence. Be as sure of your facts as possible and make notes of all points that you wish to put.

Watch out for personal prejudices and involve your boss (and possibly colleagues) beforehand to check out the objectivity and appropriateness of your approach. This is vital even at the early stages of the disciplinary procedure. It's a good idea to involve Personnel prior to any discipline likely to result in a written warning.

Arrange an interview

It is essential that all discipline is handled face-to-face and in private. Whereas it is sometimes possible to chivvy someone in front of others, any reprimand must be given 'off the job'. This means a disciplinary interview to deal with the issues. Beg, borrow or steal an office out of view and earshot and arrange not to be disturbed. For informal discipline (a verbal reprimand) this is likely to be a one-to-one meeting, but you may still want to call on others as witnesses. For more serious discipline, it might be appropriate for your boss to sit in. Make sure that the individual knows about the disciplinary procedure and any right to be accompanied by a fellow employee or other representative.

At the interview, the employee should be informed of the complaint and what the supporting evidence is. In conducting the interview, always show concern but remain unemotional.

Give a hearing

Give the person every opportunity to explain. A disciplinary interview is a two-way process, not a one-sided harangue. This is an important part of the investigation. Consider the validity of the reasons given and if new facts are brought to light, you may need to adjourn and investigate these as quickly as possible. Consider how far the individual was to blame and whether there are mitigating circumstances.

Determine the appropriate remedy

When all the relevant facts have been aired, decide what has been done wrong and what is necessary to improve the individual's conduct or performance. Develop an action plan accordingly.

Also determine carefully what level of discipline is appropriate. Take into account:

- All the facts. Don't be swayed by emotion, popular opinion or pressure. Base your decision on all the facts of the case. Give the benefit of the doubt on circumstantial evidence.

- Previous 'record'. There may have been previous warnings which need to be taken into account.

- Mitigating circumstances. This might make the action more excusable and subject to less severe discipline. Are length of service and age a consideration?

- Aggravating circumstances. The individual might be in a position which makes the action less excusable or may have compounded the problem in other ways.

Give a Hearing

- Consistency. What action has been taken on similar cases in the past? (Seek guidance from Personnel here.)

You will also need to determine the duration of the disciplinary warning. In some cases, it might be appropriate to 'wipe the slate clean' after a period of satisfactory conduct or performance in the future. Make it clear if this is to be the case.

Summarise and identify the next steps

At the end of the interview summarise:

- What the individual did wrong.

- What disciplinary action is being taken. Explain whether the warning is 'off the record' or a formal warning under the Disciplinary Procedure.

- Make clear what needs to be done to improve.

- Specify any time limits agreed for performance or conduct to be reviewed.

- Identify what the next step in the Procedure will be if there is a repetition or no improvement.

- Outline what the Appeals Procedure is.

Commit things to writing

Keep an on-going record of all situations which are likely to result in disciplinary action and record events whilst they are fresh in your mind. Keep this evidence on file and always make a note of the disciplinary meeting itself. Don't write down anything that you're not prepared to copy to the individual or which might unfairly prejudice that person in the future.

Put down the date of any verbal warning in your diary and give the individual a copy of any written warning after the disciplinary interview. Do not do this before as this defeats the object of giving a hearing. The warning letter should spell out the points outlined in the above section. Clear the wording of all written warnings with your boss and Personnel beforehand.

Follow-up

Monitor the individual constructively throughout the review period. No further formal action should be taken during this time unless things deteriorate even further or some other serious misconduct occurs.

Ensure that you re-interview when the time limit has been reached. If progress is unsatisfactory, take the appropriate formal action. Otherwise, praise the progress made and encourage this to be maintained.

Avoid grievances

This is really about trying to manage your people's concerns, problems and complaints so that there is no need for a formal grievance to be raised. However, at the end of the day, an individual may still not be satisfied with the answer that you've given and may wish to take things further. That is what a Grievance Procedure is for but, before this happens, **make sure that you have done everything you can to resolve the matter**. This is the guiding principle in avoiding grievances, so:

Anticipate concerns

Try to develop a 'sixth sense' so that you know what is likely to be a problem and of concern to your people. If possible, eliminate the difficulties in advance and always explain the reasons for things.

This approach also means always thinking through how your actions and decisions will be perceived and received. Wherever possible, consult your people beforehand to sound out their views, ideas and opinions. Take account of these if you can. It can also be useful to use your colleagues and boss as a sounding board to get reaction on what you intend to do.

Concerns and issues can also arise after the event, so keep close to how things have gone and how people are reacting. Try to cultivate an environment where people let you know what they think without you having to ask (but keep an ear to the ground anyway!).

Listen effectively

Whether people are giving feedback or raising concerns, show interest and listen effectively. It's particularly important when handling a grievance that you understand what the real issue is. Rather than argue with the individual, probe and paraphrase what is being said and summarise so that at least you are both in agreement on this. Don't promise anything at this stage but do make it clear what you will be doing next.

Act quickly and follow-up

It is then up to you to progress and attempt to resolve the issue or concern. Any unfairness or injustice needs to be put right. If you realise that you can't sort out the problem yourself, involve your boss. Investigate and use your initiative to sort things out on the individual's behalf. Make this a priority and ensure that you fix a date to go back to the person quickly.

It is vital to respond, even if nothing has changed. Try to explain things fully, so that even if the individual cannot accept the reasons, at least the position is understood.

Finally, check out whether the person is 'happy' and feels everything possible has been said or done. Clarify if any outstanding points remain to be resolved. Is there anything more that you could reasonably do?

Checklist 5

Managing Discipline and Grievances

Discipline Fairly

- Identify the standards required
- Know and follow the Disciplinary Procedure
- Act promptly
- Investigate and consult beforehand
- Give a hearing
- Determine the appropriate remedy
- Summarise and identify next steps
- Commit things to writing
- Follow up

Avoid Grievances

- Anticipate concerns
- Listen effectively
- Act quickly and follow up

6 MANAGING RECRUITMENT

Every Manager is involved in recruitment at some time and you should be aiming to appoint only high quality people who match the requirements of the job.

The following summary of best practice may help when you are involved in any recruitment.

Determine your needs

It is essential to think things through at the outset.

The first question to determine is whether you need to recruit at all. People are expensive and a vacancy is an opportunity to review whether the job is really necessary. It may also be beneficial to reorganise or redesign the job to improve productivity or create a development opportunity for an existing person. As a result, you may have no vacancy or a relatively junior one which should be easier to fill.

If you decide to recruit, raise a Staff Requisition to confirm the need and get it authorised appropriately.

Write up the job in terms of its main tasks and responsibilities. This does not have to be in the form of a traditional job description but, if one is available, so much the better. A Job Specification helps everyone to understand the job – you, Personnel, agencies and, most important of all, candidates. If the job is new or has been changed, you will also need to arrange for the grade to be determined from the Job Specification.

Having defined the job, you then need to determine the characteristics that you are looking for in the person who will carry out the job. The Person Specification should identify the skills, knowledge and experience required to do the job. Be as precise as possible and avoid words like 'bright', 'capable' and 'self starter' if you can!

The process of writing the Job and Person Specification is very important. It usually helps to clarify in your own mind what you are looking for. Unless you have done this, you are unlikely to find it!

Plan your campaign

Recruitment is costly as well as a time-consuming and lengthy process. If you know that you are going to recruit, it is advisable to get started early as the process rarely takes less than two months.

It is also vital to plan the whole approach to the campaign at the outset. This will usually be in conjunction with Personnel and is likely to involve aspects such as:

- Timescales
- Whether to recruit internally or externally (or both)
- How and when to communicate to your people (ideally before the ad appears!)
- Selection of advertising media or agency
- Production of recruitment literature, brochures, etc
- Pre-selection criteria and procedures
- Responsibility for first and second interviews.

Planning the campaign up-front helps things run smoothly and keeps costs down. It also gives you a good idea of the resource required and how much of your own and others' time you will need to set aside. In some cases, a 'full-time' co-ordinator might even be required.

Aid self-selection

Recruitment is the process of attracting candidates. Do this by presenting the job positively and objectively but without over-selling.

Try to provide sufficient initial information to enable the person to decide whether or not they are likely to meet the specification for the job. This will reduce the number of inappropriate applications and save time and administration.

You then own it to candidates to give as full an understanding of the company and the job as possible, including the demands and benefits of working there. During the selection process it often helps to show people where they would be working and to meet other people who are already working there. Overall, your aim should be to educate and be open with candidates. This enables people to select themselves in or out depending on whether things are right for them.

It is important to attract candidates for the right reasons, so don't hint at 'bigger and better things' in the future unless you are very sure that it is appropriate. There is little to be gained in recruiting a person who is over-qualified for the immediate job unless this is likely to grow or there is a specific need for that potential in the near future. No one should feel subsequently that they were ill-informed or misled by 'promises' at recruitment.

Select thoroughly

The decision to appoint is ultimately yours. To make sure that it is the right one, you need as much relevant data as you can get from interviews and other sources. Also involve and confer with others to validate your judgement and get a second opinion.

Adopt a professional approach to selection. Ensure that everyone involved in interviewing has been trained in basic skills before they are turned loose on an unsuspecting candidate.

Select Thoroughly

Key do's and don'ts which apply to selection interviewing are:

- Don't stress the candidate. The interview should be a fairly pleasant experience for everyone involved

- Plan what you want to cover and watch the time

- Ask open questions which avoid 'Yes/No' answers

- Listen and stay alert

- Keep probing relevant aspects until you fully understand

- Make it a two-way process by encouraging questions and comments from the candidate.

If you are interviewing with somebody else, plan what you are each going to cover and don't overpower the candidate with quick-fire questions. Avoid the person having to endure too many interviews and meeting a succession of people at all levels. This leaves the individual bewildered, exhausted and probably unimpressed as a result of repetitive questions.

For many jobs, interviewing is not the only way of gathering information on the suitability of the candidate. Additional possibilities might be to:

- Use relevant tests to give a broader picture of the individual. However, remember that test scores in isolation can mislead, so use them to help your overall judgement rather than to make the appointment decision for you.

- Organise an exercise which simulates some aspect of the job, particularly if specific skills are necessary, for example, writing, numeracy, keyboard skills, oral presentation, and so on.

- Describe a typical job-related problem to the candidate and ask how the person would tackle or approach it.

- Ask to be shown a piece of work of which the person is particularly proud. This gives a good idea of the individual's ability and standards – but make sure that you ascertain whether other people have been involved!

Treat people considerately

Candidates make judgements on how you treat them and their job application. In the recruitment process, you are the 'shop window' of the organisation. You need to leave people feeling good about the treatment they have received whatever the outcome for them and that applies equally to internal candidates. To achieve this, it is important to:

- Respect confidentiality at all times.

- Be courteous and tactful. Look after interviewees as 'guests' and help people relax and feel at home.

- Personalise communications. Make use of the 'phone and write in a friendly style. Don't 'force-fit' standard letters which don't match the circumstances.

- Ensure that administration is prompt and efficient. Acknowledge correspondence and thank people for their interest.

- Don't keep people hanging on. If there are delays, make contact and say so, explaining why if possible.

- Give candidates ample opportunity to ask questions and 'sell' themselves at interview. Always close by asking if there are any other aspects that the person would like to cover.

- Avoid raising expectations by strongly expressing interest or dropping broad hints at interview unless you are really likely to offer the candidate the job.

- Help people feel good about themselves. Try to reject a candidate 'positively'. For example, refer to a strong short list rather than any personal inadequacies. Congratulate and enthuse to those you offer!

Offer appropriately

Follow the advice of old campaigners – if there is any real doubt about a candidate, don't offer at all.

However, when you have found the right candidate, it's obviously vital to make the right offer.

It's always useful to explore current remuneration and expectations of short-listed candidates in order to get a broad idea of what is likely to be acceptable. You then need to pitch the offer right in relation to job rate and the salaries of existing staff. Don't pay less than the person is worth because their existing package is significantly below your organisation's standards or go over the top to provide an incentive to join. Both extremes are likely to give you differential problems which may linger over two or three subsequent Salary Reviews. If there is any doubt about the acceptability of the grade or the package, sound out the candidate and talk to Personnel on the offer before making a final decision.

By all means offer verbally when this is likely to help acceptance. However, always make this subject to satisfactory medical reports and employment references, and follow-up with a written offer from Personnel as soon as possible. Don't pressurise too soon for an answer – give people reasonable time to think.

Keep in touch with the person after the offer has been accepted and confirmed. It will probably be appreciated if you send off any snippets of relevant news or information, offer help and arrange to meet during a pre-employment visit, or just ring to enquire how things are going whilst the person is waiting to join.

Finally, make sure that you've organised everything for when the new starter arrives – from workstation to induction plan. That's an essential part of a warm welcome.

Checklist 6

Managing Recruitment

- Determine your needs
- Plan your campaign
- Aid self-selection
- Select thoroughly
- Treat people considerately
- Offer appropriately

7 MANAGING REWARD

Your overall objective here is to ensure that everyone is treated consistently and gets a fair deal for their contribution. To achieve this the key activities for you are to recognise people's contribution and reward fairly.

Recognise contribution

Recognition is a fundamental part of managing reward. Don't underestimate its importance and remember that a word of encouragement, thanks, and praise from you can often mean as much to a person as any monetary reward. Just by recognising an individual's contribution, you can help bring a sense of satisfaction and achievement as well as generate commitment for the future.

The three golden rules on recognition are:

- **Make sure that you do it.**
- **Don't overdo it.**
- **Always be genuine.**

Reward fairly

Everyone's reward must be fair in relation to others and in proportion to individual contribution.

In practice, this means that you need a good working know-ledge of the job evaluation system(s) which apply to your staff as well as the process by which market-related salaries are established and individual salaries are determined. At some time you will need to explain various points on these subjects

Reward Fairly

to others, so if there are gaps in your own knowledge or understanding, ask your Manager or Personnel for help now.

To reward fairly, you then need to:

Match grade to job size

Ensure that each person is always correctly graded for the job being undertaken. That involves being conscientious on keeping job descriptions up to date and ensuring that new and changed jobs are evaluated to determine grade as soon as possible. It's up to you to initiate these job evaluation requests and keep the 'System' in good repair.

When the job is correctly graded, you then need to determine whether the individual is performing at the minimum level expected for the full job. Remember that promotion is about doing a bigger job and is not just a reward for good performance. In this respect, the timing of promotion is vitally important. Promoting too early can result in too much pressure on the individual to perform, whilst leaving it too late can lead to frustration and injustice. Be clear in your own mind on the justification for each promotion and ask yourself whether this is likely to be perceived as fair by the individual and others likely to have a view.

Relate total reward to performance

Always use performance as the yardstick for determining an individual's position within the salary range. Generally, people with average, competent performance should be paid at or around the mid-point of the grade. Individuals whose performance is well above average should be paid in the top half of the range, whilst those who are less experienced or whose performance is below average should be paid in the bottom half of the range.

When you've established an individual's salary in the right position within the range, test whether the league table of salaries for all your people is correct. You need to be happy both with the position of each salary against job rate and relative to all others.

Finally, ensure that an individual's overall earnings reflect extra performance rather than just additional hours. For that reason, overtime working should always be authorised as being necessary in advance.

Aim for understanding

If people are to feel fairly rewarded, they need to have some understanding of the basis on which their grade and salary are determined. Every individual needs to know where they stand on grade and salary and you should be in a position to explain the reasons behind this if the need arises.

If an individual does raise a problem or concern on remuneration, be prepared to discuss and investigate this (involving Personnel if appropriate). You should always be able to provide an explanation, even though it may not be the answer that the person wants.

One final point to bear in mind when talking to people about remuneration is to respect the confidentiality of other people's salary details.

Stay objective

Try to remain as logical and dispassionate as possible when you are involved in rewarding others. Remember that you are likely to create problems for yourself if you:

- View your own people as 'swans' and everyone else's as 'geese'. Beware the halo effect.

- Blame the Job Evaluation system or Salary Policy for not delivering what the individual wants. "Of course, if it was left to me . . ."

- Pay people the same regardless of their performance in case there is likely to be a reaction.

- Give merit increases for sustained rather than improved performance.

- Make promises and offer 'carrots' which it may not be possible to deliver.

Make sure that you stay objective by getting the views of others wherever possible rather than relying solely on your own judgement. It can help to get feedback from your boss and others on the size of the job or the performance of an individual when you are thinking about a Job Evaluation submission or a Salary Review recommendation. Also check out your own recommendations with the views of other Managers and Personnel when there is a need for consistency and equity of treatment across areas. Always consider the wider implications of how you want to reward your people.

Checklist 7

Managing Reward

Recognise Contribution

- Do it
- Don't overdo it
- Always be genuine

Reward Fairly

- Match grade to job size
- Relate total reward to performance
- Aim for understanding
- Stay objective

8 MANAGING TRAINING AND DEVELOPMENT

To manage training and development effectively, you need to be clear about what you are trying to achieve. The guiding principles should always be to help people improve their performance and realise their full abilities.

With this as your focus, training becomes more than just booking your people on courses or seeing their development in terms of the next promotion. When the objective is better performance, providing proper training and supporting individual development are ongoing management activities which are essential rather than 'nice to do'.

Provide proper training

The training of your people is your responsibility. You should determine the training needed, how and when it is to be given, and identify how far performance has improved as a result. Often you will be the best person to carry out training - but, even when you are not the trainer, it is still a key part of your management role to make sure that training is provided.

Plan training

Plan your time so that you can give the right attention to training others. Resist the temptation to ignore training responsibilities or to rush any training that you give in order to get back to 'more pressing' priorities. If you don't ensure that people receive proper training to acquire the necessary skills and knowledge, you will spend your time doing, checking and correcting their work and replacing people who have left. This vicious circle means that you will be even busier and under more pressure than if you had given proper training in the first place.

Always think through what training is required. This means establishing training needs and developing an appropriate training plan.

- **Establish training needs**

    People's needs vary – from new starters fresh to the job to existing employees who need additional skills and knowledge to improve performance. As a Manager, it is up to you to identify what key activities the job involves, what skills and knowledge the person already possesses and where training is required. Remember that effective training is providing what people need, which is not necessarily the same as what they want.

- **Develop an individual training plan**

    Having identified what people need to know or do, the next step is to plan how and when this is best achieved. A Training Plan can cover a few weeks or several years and is essentially a series of building blocks of training and experience designed to meet an individual's needs. Don't just restrict yourself to courses – training can encompass induction, on-the-job training, coaching and counselling, job rotation, projects and so on.

    Establish a written plan for each individual covering what training is needed, when and how this is going to be achieved, and record when this has been done. Whatever training methods are used, a systematic, planned approach to training is essential. You need to be able to tell at a glance what training is needed, what has been achieved and who is trained to do what in your area.

Help people learn

Learning is a voluntary process and you can have a major impact in motivating your people to learn by:

- Showing the right attitude yourself. Push the benefits of training and allow time for it. Never imply that learning is 'non work' or that time devoted to it is unproductive. Share your own knowledge and experience and make it easy for people to educate themselves by circulating information and items of interest.

- Making sure that there is a positive pay-off from learning. People need to feel that training is meaningful and appreciate the benefits for them. Make it easy to relate the training to the work situation and ensure that people understand the relevance to their success.

- Building confidence. People who are learning are usually self-conscious and make mistakes. Show encouragement by emphasising what they have done right rather than wrong. Stress what they should have done and don't harp on the mistake. Never allow people in a learning situation to feel intimidated, ridiculed or patronised. However, be discriminating in your praise – reserve that as a reward for effort and success.

Provide thorough induction

It is your responsibility to introduce newcomers to your area. Help them settle quickly and feel at home by following a planned induction programme.

- Develop a checklist which covers all the topics which the person needs to know about.

- Make sure that all the details of the person's work area are finalised before arrival and arrange a proper schedule of training and meeting people.

- Don't overload a new person with too much information too soon. This only tends to confuse and increase anxiety.

- Keep in close contact after the formal induction is over. Lack of confidence and self doubt can arise a few weeks or months into a new job and lead to 'post-induction' crisis.

Develop the right attitude

Attitudes can't be 'learned' in quite the same way as skills and knowledge. However, you can generate high commitment and morale in your team by encouraging a positive attitude.

Developing the right attitude means ensuring that your people understand and appreciate the way in which you want them to do the job, behave and work with other people. This is really a process of education which begins at induction and needs to be expanded and reinforced thereafter by yourself. This doesn't mean 'brainwashing', but it is important to encourage everyone to take a pride in what they do, to achieve high standards, and to value an atmosphere that is based on trust.

Give effective instruction

People do develop skills and knowledge by experience, but will usually become competent more quickly if this is assisted by proper instruction. It is up to you to provide the training that people need to do their job. Don't let them 'sink or swim' or have to pick things up 'as they go along'. You need to provide effective instruction on what to do and how to do it.

When you are in the role of Trainer-Manager (i.e. doing the training), it is also useful to follow some simple guidelines which help people learn effectively:

- **Know your trainee**

  Trainees learn better at their own pace. Ascertain the level of skill, knowledge and experience of the person and gear your training to this. Adjust your approach to meet an individual's needs and abilities.

- **Structure your material**

  Order your material and break up what you are teaching into digestible chunks which link sensibly.

  Before you go on from one chunk to the next, make sure that the learning has been absorbed.

- **Use effective methods**

  Always try to make training interesting, entertaining and meaningful. Use familiar examples and avoid jargon. Demonstrate what is required and employ as many visual aids as possible to augment 'theoretical' material. Trainees learn best by doing – give them as much real life practice as possible. Remember "I hear and forget, I see and remember, I do and understand".

- **Concentrate on positive instruction**

  Avoid negative instruction. Only talk about and demonstrate the right way.

- **Give feedback on performance quickly and frequently**

  This serves two purposes. First, as information on how the trainee is doing and what to do differently; second, as praise and encouragement.

- **Follow up**

  Reinforce learning by giving something to read or something to practice on. Sample and quality check from time to time to ensure that everything has been understood.

Coach

Coaching is part of your job. It is the personal help which you give to improve aspects of your people's performance and attitude. Coaching is a continuous process which helps people who are already quite competent to find solutions to current work problems and develop specific skills.

Coaching can happen whenever you or the individual think it will help. To coach effectively you need to:

- Know enough about the person and their work to be able to offer helpful guidance and support.
- Develop a plan and set goals and targets against which to review progress.
- Provide help as necessary but avoid giving instant advice and answers. This can lead to resentment.
- Try to guide the person to discover what to do for themselves as this produces commitment to the solution.

Use courses selectively

Off-the-job training can be very useful when it meets the needs of the individual. Courses are usually ready-made and easy to arrange, but resist the temptation to send people on courses because 'they are there'. Remember that there may be cheaper and more effective ways by which people can be trained and learn. First, consider whether the content and timing of a course is appropriate and then help your people get the most out of off-the-job training. Examine the course objectives to ensure that the individual is likely to get value from them. Then discuss these objectives and agree precisely what the person should be aiming to achieve from the course.

Evaluate training given

Hold a review on return from the course to discover how things went and discuss how new learning can be translated into improved performance.

It is also important to follow up whether training has worked and been worthwhile. Don't confuse evaluating effectiveness with people liking the training. Whilst it does matter that the instruction was proficient and the course admin. was efficient, the key issue is whether the training has improved performance. To check effectiveness, ask yourself two questions:

Use Courses Selectively

- **What is the person doing differently as a result?**

  Look at behaviour. Has there been any change? Has the amount of help which the person requires reduced? Are error rates lower and have quality standards improved? Are objectives and targets met more easily? Has flexibility or versatility increased? Overall, is performance more effective?

- **Was it worth it?**

  Is the training producing returns through improved quality and business performance? Use a simple measure like how much time is this training saving. As a very rough rule of thumb, if training isn't saving any time, it's unlikely to be making any other savings.

Support individual development

You need to be commited to development. This is a broad process which includes extending skills and knowledge or acquiring new and different experience. Development isn't necessarily about promotion or salary progression.

Ensure that people's abilities are used to the full. Development is a shared responsibility for the advantage of the person and organisation and it is up to you to help realise talent and potential. We owe that to everybody and it makes good business sense.

Commitment to development means that you should:

Help self development

Self-initiated development is to be commended and supported. You might be able to.

- Help people understand themselves better. Sensitive and

objective feedback can help identify an individual's strengths and weaknesses and overcome personal blocks to progress.

- Provide the right climate for self-development. This ranges from reinforcing the self discipline needed by an individual through to recognising achievements.

- Advise on the best strategy for self improvement, i.e. the direction in which to develop and when and how to acquire the necessary learning and experience.

Use people's abilities fully

Try to ensure that there is sufficient opportunity for your people to use as many of their abilities as possible to best effect in the job that you give them. Beside using resources effectively, this helps people grow and avoids a feeling of wasted talent. However, it is important to get the balance right. Don't overstretch by demanding more than the individual can deliver.

Discuss aspirations

It is important for your people to feel that you know and are interested in their aspirations and take these into account wherever possible. At Performance Appraisal and on other suitable occasions, you should discuss and record the direction in which people want to gain experience and develop. Explain that knowing this will help you to structure work and experience appropriately and consider the person for any opportunity which might arise. Find out what the individual would like to do without raising expectations or making any promises. Try to modify any aspirations which are totally unrealistic.

Establish a development process

You need to regularly review how best to match the aspirations and development needs of all your people with possible opportunities and operating requirements within your area.

This is an essential management process and you need to put time aside to do this regularly (probably once or twice a year). Obtaining a best fit is difficult. As a result you may not always be able to please everyone, especially as achieving your business objectives must remain first priority.

Whether you tackle this process as an individual Manager or as part of a management team (or both), you should:

- Go for approaches which both improve effectiveness and create development opportunities; for example, cross-training and rotation provide interest for individuals as well as increasing flexibility.

- Generate opportunities through job design, new positions, projects and organisational change which help people to grow and also improve productivity.

- Work on general career direction. A more detailed career plan for an individual can be quickly overtaken by new opportunities and a variety of other considerations.

- Try to structure experience so that it serves the interest of individual as well as operational requirements.

- Identify any really talented individuals who would respond to fast development (and then provide it).

- Think carefully before you make any specific commitment to anybody on their next move or job as a result of this process. Can you deliver?

Grow your own

Growing your own is visible commitment to development and, wherever you can, it makes good sense to fill jobs from within.

The ideal is to spot talented individuals and help them to develop the necessary skills and experience to be ready for opportunities when they arise. 'The right people in the right place at the right time'. In practice, things can't usually be planned that precisely. Your prime candidate may not be

Grow Your Own

ready or available or there may not be anybody remotely suitable for the position.

However, if there is any element of choice, think hard before going outside. Existing people can develop much faster than anticipated given a real challenge and the right support. You are likely to have more reliable information about internal candidates. It might also be possible to reorganise so that the full job does not need to be undertaken at once. Overall, there are usually fewer risks in 'Picking Your Own' than appointing externally. Remember that if you do have to recruit outside for whatever reason, it's important that your people know in advance (possibly by circulating the advertisement) and understand the reasons for this.

Take a broad view

Grow people for the organisation and not just for your own area. Approach development corporately rather than as a parochial process. By adopting this wider perspective, you maximise opportunities for your people and will attract talented individuals who see your team as a good place to develop and grow.

- Make sure that you publicise opportunities elsewhere and that your people understand that there is no stigma in seeking a transfer through the proper channels.

- Regard replacement as a development opportunity. Don't be unreasonable on transfer dates for an individual who has been offered a move.

- Never off-load problem people or poor performers on to others. It's up to you to tackle these problems yourself and you will lose credibility if you disguise 'dumping' as development.

- Plan and develop proper succession to enable people to move when their abilities and interests would be furthered elsewhere (which might be outside the organisation on occasions). This avoids such individuals becoming trapped and the development of others being blocked.

- Identify competent and talented individuals who are ready for a move and would benefit from experience outside your area. Help such people by flagging this up and discussing possibilities for a move with your boss, colleagues and/or Personnel.

- Create and identify opportunities within your area which might suit the development of people from elsewhere. Publicise these appropriately and don't poach or directly approach individuals from other areas. Always discuss an opportunity with their Manager first.

Checklist 8

Managing Training and Development

Provide Proper Training

- Plan training
- Help people learn
- Provide thorough induction
- Develop the right attitude
- Give effective instruction
- Coach performance
- Use courses selectively
- Evaluate training given

Support Individual Development

- Help self-development
- Use abilities fully
- Discuss aspirations
- Establish a development process
- Grow your own
- Take a broad view

9 MANAGING COMMUNICATION

To a large extent, your effectiveness as a Manager and a leader will depend upon how well you communicate.

Whatever the direction of that communication (downwards, upwards or laterally), your objective should always be the same – to ensure understanding. When people understand, communication has been effective and improved performance, motivation and involvement should follow. This section covers the essentials of what you need to do to be an effective communicator.

Develop your communication skills

Try to become an 'all-round' communicator. This means understanding something about all the basic communication skills and putting them into practice. There are courses and booklets to help and it is only appropriate here to summarise a few pointers.

Present effectively

Whether you are briefing your team in an informal way or faced with a nerve-racking public presentation, the approach to verbal presentations is the same:

- First, think through the single most important result that you want from the presentation. What is your prime objective?

- Know your audience. What is the best way of getting your message across and how long have you got?

- Do your homework. Gather all the information that you need to put your message across. Distil this into no more than half a dozen key ideas.

- Develop a logical structure to put the message over.

- Play Devil's Advocate. What sort of objections and questions are you likely to encounter? What is the best way of dealing with them?

- Think how best to gain the attention of your audience. Do you need any visual aids to help?

- Rehearse and practise giving presentations as often as you can. Find the style that suits you best (and don't forget to smile!).

- Always check the time, venue and setting for your presentation and that everything you need is there (and works).

Write thoughtfully

The first question to address is whether or not to put things down in writing. It may be that phoning or a face-to-face meeting is more appropriate and quicker. Only write things down if you:

- Want a record for the future

- Want to confirm an understanding

- Want to ensure clarity and/or accountability

- Want to analyse something

- Want a considered reply.

If you need to write, be concise and don't waste the reader's time. Remember that 'One Page Memos' are likely to be read and actioned rather than put aside for 'later'.

Written work gives an impression of you watch out for accuracy, spelling and errors. That doesn't mean that everything has to be typed. Don't overlook the effectiveness of a handwritten request or response.

Listen carefully

This can really help to improve your impact as a Manager. The benefits of listening are two-way – if you listen to other people, the chances are that they will listen to you.

Follow the Ten Commandments of Good Listening:

- Stop talking! You can't listen if you are talking.

- Put the talker at ease. Help the person feel free to talk.

- Show the talker that you want to listen. Look and act interested. Don't read your mail while the other person talks.

- Remove distractions. Don't doodle, tap or shuffle papers.

- Empathise with the talker. Try to put yourself in the talker's place so you can see that point of view.

- Be patient. Allow plenty of time and don't interrupt.

- Control your temper. An angry person often gets the wrong meaning.

- Go easy on argument and criticism. This puts the talker on the defensive. Don't argue – even if you win, you lose.

- Ask questions. This encourages the talker and shows that you are listening.

- Stop talking! This is first and last, because all other commandments depend upon it.

Read selectively

Reading is part of your job. There are courses available to help you read faster but it is also important to organise your reading.

Put time aside to read each day but be selective. First decide what needs to be read (skim/scan). Then decide in what depth (fast read and highlight for information; slow read and take notes for comprehension).

Read Selectively

Keep others informed

It requires self discipline on your part to do this. Ensure that you get the right balance between communicating to your boss, your team and other people across the organisation. Don't concentrate on communicating in one direction at the expense of others, for example, by keeping your boss in the picture but not letting your team know what's happening. To keep others informed, it is important to:

Establish a system

Two key aspects of communication are remembering to do it and making it easy to do. If you develop drills and systems, this can help in both respects. First, think through what you regularly need to do to keep people informed. Then set up the mechanics to make this happen.

Diarise progress meetings with your Manager and the people reporting to you. Arrange communication meetings with your people and liaison meetings with other departments for some months ahead. This ensures that communication doesn't get forgotten or overlooked.

Keeping others informed may call for regular reports and information to be produced and circulated. Determine who needs what and why and set up procedures to provide this.

Develop standard distribution lists wherever you can, but from time to time review whether the copies are used or needed.

Finally, don't overlook the local notice board system as a means of communicating. Make someone accountable for regularly updating the board.

Aim for understanding

Try to communicate in a way that ensures your message is understood. A useful tip here is always to put yourself in the position of your audience. Keep in mind the need to:

- **Be relevant**

  Make sure that what you communicate to people relates to what they want and need to know and that you are not just 'dumping' information on them. This means that you may have to 'customise' the communication for the particular audience. Highlight the essentials and keep it short and simple (KISS) to make things easy for people to understand.

- **Be timely**

  The timing of your communication is often as important as the content. You need to ensure that people find out things first from you as their Manager rather than by getting to hear first through the grapevine. To achieve this, you have to plan and co-ordinate how and when to communicate. Wherever possible, ensure that you consult or inform people about matters directly affecting them before the information becomes general knowledge. They may need to keep what you tell them confidential for a period, but your trust is inevitably appreciated and respected.

  Finally, make sure that your boss finds out about issues and complaints concerning your area from you rather than somebody else.

- **Be honest**

  Don't just be a 'Good News' Manager. You need to communicate in such a way that people appreciate where they stand and how things are going. Don't breach confidentiality or demotivate or hurt people unnecessarily, but be objective and honest or your credibility as a Manager will be lost.

- **Check understanding**

  Perceptions of what has been said can vary and emphasis

can be distorted in transmission. Check out that what you have communicated has been received and understood.

Do this by making communication sessions two-way and ask for questions and feedback on topics. If necessary, summarise the key points that you have put across and/or confirm these in writing. When you are communicating to your people through other Managers, ensure that the message has been received and understood all the way down the line. Ask a few people at random about what they have been told (or not!) to check grass roots understanding.

Brief your team

Team Briefing is a useful communication drill which is two-way and can be used for a variety of information, both on a regular and *ad hoc* basis. It is important to brief your team personally and written communication is no substitute for this.

- Team Briefers do it face-to-face. This ensures understanding and provides explanation. It allows dialogue and feedback on issues of relevance.

- Keep the group to a reasonable size. Around four to twelve is about right for useful two-way communication.

- Prepare the Brief. Distil the essentials from the Company briefing note and include your own local information. Work on a 50/50 Company and local split, plus time for questions.

- Keep it brief. A regular session should last about half an hour and be short and snappy.

Keep yourself in touch

Managers who are 'remote' can easily lose control of what is going on. You need to develop an approach which keeps you close to your area without interfering unnecessarily. It is also important for your people to feel that their Manager is 'around' and interested. To keep yourself in touch, you need to:

Encourage openness

You should know about the views and opinions of your people as well as what is happening. Create an atmosphere which encourages people to be open and to raise issues or problems which concern them. At least then you are in a position to do something about it. Encourage openness by showing interest in your people and ensuring that there are no penalties for speaking up or giving constructive criticism.

Be accessible

This doesn't mean that your door always needs to be open but try to work near your team and do try and see people when they ask if you've got a moment. There should be a minimum of formality or fuss for people who want to see you face-to-face. (Make sure that your secretary understands that is how you want things.)

Be visible

Your people will be reassured and motivated if you make the effort to visit them from time to time. It demonstrates that what they are doing matters and that you are interested and involved. 'Walking the job' is important and you need to approach this in the right way, which is to:

- Have a purpose. Aimlessly wandering around in a transparent attempt to socialise wastes everyone's time and makes people uneasy.

- Make it regular. Sudden 'one-off' appearances just cause worry. "What's wrong now?"

- Educate yourself. This is an opportunity to find out what individuals do, what problems exist and whether wider issues are understood.

Be Visible

- Tell people what's happening and what you do. It is an opportunity to keep them informed.

When you Manage by Walking About, you can also jump a level and talk directly to the people who report to your Managers. 'Leap frog' sessions like these can be very useful for everyone involved – but make sure that the Manager concerned knows why you are doing this.

Manage meetings

You need to ensure that the meetings that you call and run are productive – both in use of time and outcome. Key points to remember are to:

Plan

This includes determining whether you really need a meeting to achieve what has to be done. Identify the purpose of the meeting, the topics to be covered and the fewest possible number of people who need to be involved.

Prepare

Issue a self-explanatory agenda or some form of written programme for the meeting. Identify the order of items and how much time is available for each. Attach any material which needs to be read beforehand and use 'pre-meetings' to save time if necessary.

Chair

Run the meeting in a businesslike way and arrange for a record to be taken. Keep the discussion on track and on time. Avoid covering issues twice, control private discussions and involve everyone.

Record

Summarise conclusions and record decisions. Produce notes and minutes with action points and responsibilities.

Managing Communication

Develop Your Communication Skills

- Present effectively
- Write thoughtfully
- Listen carefully
- Read selectively

Keep Others Informed

- Establish a system
- Aim for understanding
- Brief your team

Keep Yourself in Touch

- Encourage openness
- Be accessible
- Be visible

Manage Meetings

- Plan
- Prepare
- Chair
- Record

10 MANAGING ORGANISATION

The 'right organisation' is the one which meets business needs best. As a result, there are a number of different types and mixtures of organisation based on specialist functions, products or projects. It is up to each area to determine which type of organisation is most appropriate to deliver the results required. However, within this overall flexibility, we all need to ensure that the organisation which reports to us is effective both in terms of structure and the way people operate within it. To manage your organisation effectively, you need to:

Develop an appropriate structure

Think about your organisation structure in terms of Chains of Command, Spans of Control and Accountability. Try to:

Minimise levels

Aim for the fewest layers of management possible. Short chains of command assist rapid and accurate communication (up and down the organisation) and support quick and effective decision making.

Each manager in a chain of command needs clear responsibility and the authority to make decisions. Each manager's job should be different from those of his boss and his subordinates but linked to them.

Optimise spans of control

There is no magic number of subordinates – each case must be looked at on its merits. Whether a grouping is manageable depends upon factors such as the experience of the people, the nature of the work, the amount of planning and co-ordination required by you, and so on. Generally, the more complex and/or varied the task being managed, the fewer the subordinates.

Test whether the trade-off between span of control and hierarchy is right, i.e. between the height and breadth of your organisation. A long hierarchy can bring communication failures, remoteness from decision making and too few opportunities for initiative. Too flat a structure might overstretch management and not allow time for people to be managed properly. It's all a matter of getting the right balance!

Ensure clear accountability

Your organisation will work best if there is a clear reporting structure and people understand their role and responsibilities.

To help achieve this:

- Ensure that everyone involved knows to whom they report and who reports to them.

- Clearly define who is in charge. This includes who is responsible for delivering results and who can make what decisions. If you make a person responsible for achieving a specific result, you must also give sufficient power and authority to make decisions and take action.

- Keep reporting lines clear and avoid dual reporting wherever you can. Make sure that there are no gaps or overlaps to cause confusion.

- Check with customers and colleagues that responsibilities are clear looking from the outside and that interfaces work smoothly.

- As a final test, try to explain your organisation structure to somebody else unconnected with it. If it proves difficult or confusing, then perhaps your structure could be improved.

Build teams and teamwork

Small teams generate high commitment and an informal working atmosphere. The advantages are clear, so do everything that you can to organise your people into teams and encourage team working.

Team development takes time. It is usually a gradual process of growth from an initial, immature stage to the formation of a tight-knit working group. The following reminders on building an effective team might be useful:

Keep numbers tight

There are no hard and fast rules but 6 is normally the optimum for developing a really cohesive team identity. With more than about 12, a team begins to fragment.

Ensure the right mix

A team usually benefits from variety in its membership. Matching characteristics such as age and similar values can increase a team's cohesiveness but a mix of different skills, knowledge and aptitudes makes for a very productive working unit. Don't just try to put 'like with like' but build a team of people whose combined strengths suit the needs of the task.

Provide clear objectives

Strong teams share a well developed sense of common purpose. This comes from a clear understanding of what is expected from the group and a growing commitment by individuals to achieve this as a team. As Manager, it's up to you to provide these clear objectives and it will help team development to discuss, clarify and jointly agree these.

Give appropriate leadership

Teams develop powerful internal codes of behaviour and performance. Make sure that from the outset you establish (and demonstrate) the right values and standards of performance required from the team.

You are the formal team leader but effective teams are usually capable of achieving what's required themselves. When this is so, delegate and restrict your role to co-ordination and providing the right level of resources. It might also be appropriate for other team members to exercise an informal leadership role within the group at times when their specific skills make this appropriate.

Foster team identity

Help people see themselves as part of a team and not as isolated individuals. Take every opportunity to get your people working in the same place, training as a team, meeting together regularly and socialising as a group. All this helps build team identity and don't forget that it is also very important to recognise team as well as individual achievement.

Keep competition constructive

Teams can get very self-centred because of internal loyalty and commitment to team goals. Some competition between teams can be productive, but don't let this get out of hand. Too much competition can lead to deteriorating relationships and wasted time and effort. Always stress that teams need to work together to achieve shared objectives.

Aim for organisational effectiveness

Having built the organisation, you should continually work to develop its effectiveness. To do this, you need to measure how

Foster Team Identity

things are going, improve performance and increase the resilience of the structure.

Measure results

Wherever you can, measure the effectiveness of your organisation by developing measures of performance, both internal and external.

The prime external measures are quality of output and client satisfaction. Always check the level of service yourself and ask users for feedback to ensure that your organisation is producing the results required.

Internal measures can also demonstrate how well an organisation structure is performing. You should develop and use appropriate yardsticks, for example:

- Check now and again on how people are spending their time. This can often give a good indication on whether the organisation is working well and people are being used in the right way.

- Track the level of absence and turnover in your area against the Company average. If absence or turnover is high or rising, make sure that you understand the reasons for this and that there is no link with an organisational issue.

- Get a fix on the level of morale and motivation in your area. For example, how high is the level of commitment, what is the volume and nature of 'grumbles', are you attracting good people from elsewhere, are your own people making satisfactory progress, and so on?

Of course, even if all is not well, that does not necessarily mean that you need to change your organisation – but at least make sure that this is not the cause of your problems.

Improve performance

It is often possible to develop the performance of your area through reorganisation. However, avoid the 'When in doubt, reorganise' approach and don't change your organisation just for the sake of it. First analyse the strengths and weaknesses of the existing structure and then plan any changes carefully, communicating to all individuals affected in good time. Unless you are sure that the new structure will be an improvement, it may be better to leave well enough alone. That said, always view your current organisation structure as offering scope for improved performance and, in particular, try to:

- **Consolidate Activities**

    Look for economies of scale by combining related activities and grouping similar functions. More specialisation can bring productivity improvements but beware of narrowing jobs to an unacceptable level. By rationalisation, you may be able to shorten the chain of command to improve the effectiveness of communication and increase the number of subordinates of people who are growing to produce bigger and more fulfilling jobs, and so on.

- **Design jobs**

    When grouping activities into jobs, try to get the best fit between productivity, cost effectiveness and the need for satisfaction by the person doing the job. Whenever you have scope, try to provide:

    - variety through different activities
    - responsibility for a whole task with a tangible outcome
    - autonomy to plan and organise work. Give as much discretion as possible on how the job should be done
    - feedback on performance and the quality of work.

All this gives meaning and responsibility to the work people do. By designing jobs in this way, you will also maximise opportunity for development within your organisation.

Design Jobs

- **Grow jobs**

  It is often possible to combine an individual's need for personal and career development with higher productivity and efficiency. You may be able to enlarge jobs by combining elements from others. Adding new tasks and activities from across the organisation increases variety. It is also possible to enrich jobs by giving capable people more responsibility and freedom to manage themselves and their work. In some situations, it might even be appropriate to develop a job and organisation structure around an individual when that meets the needs of the business and the development of the person.

Increase resilience

It's important that your organisation can withstand the changes in workload, people and other external factors which are likely to affect it. Try to anticipate likely demands in advance and think through plans and contingencies as appropriate. You will certainly need to:

- **Plan succession**

  Think through succession for each of the key jobs in your area. What are the vulnerabilities and how will you manage if the current jobholder leaves or moves immediately? Is there a prime candidate for replacement or will you need to reorganise? Then consider how your succession plan looks for the medium/long term. Amongst your people, who will be ready for what position by when? Do you need to do more to strengthen specific areas of skill, knowledge or experience by development and/or recruitment?

  Arrange a formal session with your boss at least once a year to review your organisation and succession plans. This will help identify any vulnerabilities or gaps and will also provide the benefit of a wider perspective.

  Finally, remember to plan and develop succession for yourself. It might be the only thing which is stopping your progress!

• Ensure flexibility

Develop a sufficiently broad base of experience to enable your area to operate when short-handed, for example as a result of sickness, holiday or turnover. Make sure that every key job can be covered temporarily by somebody else as and when the need arises. To achieve this, you should plan and arrange cross-training and job rotation on an ongoing basis. Although this can be marginally more expensive in terms of resource, this is usually outweighed by the advantages of having adequate cover for your foreseeable needs and being able to provide more varied work for people.

Finally, make sure that people understand the need for them to be flexible to help meet work peaks and changing priorities. When you need to move people around to keep your organisation effective, think about the impact on the individual and try to take this into account. Always make sure that the basis for selection for movement is as fair as possible and that people understand the reasons for the change.

Checklist 10

Managing Organisation

Develop an Appropriate Structure

- Minimise levels
- Optimise Spans of Control
- Ensure clear accountability

Build Teams and Teamwork

- Keep numbers tight
- Ensure the right mix
- Provide clear objectives
- Give appropriate leadership
- Foster team identity
- Keep competition constructive

Aim for Organisational Effectiveness

- Measure results
- Improve performance
- Increase resilience

11 MANAGING QUALITY

As a Manager you are accountable for the quality of service and work in your area. This means that it is a part of your job to ensure all tasks are completed consistently to a standard which meets the needs of the business. To achieve this, you need to:

- Set clear standards
- Plan how to meet those standards
- Track the quality achieved
- Take action to improve quality where necessary.

Set clear standards

To manage quality, you and your people need to have a clear and shared understanding of the standards required. However, you also need to find out from your clients what quality they expect, decide what standards should be met and communicate this effectively. Such a statement of standards will serve as a contract between you, your customers, and your team.

Consult your customers

First, identify who they are. Clearly your own Manager is one, and others may be identified by considering:

- Who are your department's objectives designed to satisfy?
- Who receives the end-products of your work?
- Who do you and your people communicate with?

Second, talk with your customers and understand better what standard of work and service they expect from you and your team. You should involve some of your people in this process to help them understand some of the wider issues.

Discuss topics such as timeliness, accuracy, presentation of work and service levels.

Talking through examples of what is and is not acceptable will help. Document these discussions and copy in your clients to ensure you have understood them correctly.

Decide on appropriate quality standards

It is your job to decide on quality standards for your department which are in the best interests of the Company. You need to take account of:

- The quality expected by your clients
- The costs and benefits of delivering different degrees of quality
- The impact of different degrees of quality on:

  - your clients and their needs
  - contribution to departmental objectives
  - your people's attitude and motivation
  - other departments.

You will need to discuss this further with your clients and team and it is likely to be an evolutionary process. However, it is important for you to get some standards in place early and refine them rather than spend a long time aiming for perfection on paper.

Communicate quality standards

Having decided on the standards, you need to make sure they are clear to your people and your customers. This will help to ensure the right standards are achieved.

Communicate Quality Standards

You need to:

- Involve your team in setting standards.

- Document the standards. Make sure that they are clear, specific, measurable and comprehensive.

- Endorse the standards. Let your staff know that you are committed to meeting this level of quality.

- Publish the standards to your people and your customers.

- Regularly discuss and reinforce your standards and the reasons for them with your staff and clients.

Review these standards

Changing business requirements may mean that standards need to change. You need to review the standards every so often to make sure they still apply. Discuss any possible changes with your people and clients before making them. In particular you should review the cost implications of making any changes.

Achieve the standards required

Having decided on appropriate quality standards you need to plan how you are going to deliver work to meet the standards. You should:

- Agree and document *procedures and methods* to meet the standards.

- Agree and document *controls* to ensure that the standards will be met. These may include checklists, registers, checkpoint meetings, authorisation procedures or other controls.

- Agree and document *responsibilities* via job descriptions and terms of reference.

- Prepare and implement **training plans** for your staff to ensure they are familiar with the standards, procedures, controls and their responsibilities.

The end result will be a documented system of how your people are expected to operate, the standards expected of them and a plan to ensure that people are capable of meeting the standards.

Once implemented, activities such as these are known as Quality Assurance in that they are intended to help you assure the quality of the work.

Track the quality achieved

After you have set up the process to achieve quality, you need an information system to know how things are going. This is Quality Control.

Install quality controls

Your Quality Control System is likely to provide a means of comparing a sample of the work completed against the standards, with some analysis and suggested action points if there are problems. It should be a simple system, recording whether individual pieces of work have met the separate standards. Make sure also that the quality control checking is done by someone other than the person doing the original work. Apply the system consistently so that any trends may be identified. Briefly summarise the results for reporting purposes.

Sound out your customers

Your clients are assessing the quality of your department's work all the time. Use this to your advantage. Encourage feedback and develop constructive action points from it.

Discuss quality with your staff

Your staff are closer to some of the problems than you are. Encourage them to discuss their problems constructively amongst themselves and with you. It can be surprising what useful information you get from asking "What are the biggest problems you have at the moment?" Discuss vulnerabilities as they see them and how these can be reduced.

Ask for an audit

See audits as an opportunity not a threat. Auditors can give you an independent opinion of the quality being achieved and the effectiveness of the procedures and controls you use. This can help you to develop your procedures and controls to achieve the quality you want.

Improve quality

When you have installed good systems to track the quality being achieved, you need to use them constructively to improve quality and work on problem areas.

Involve your staff

Your people have a huge influence on the quality of their work. You need to gain their commitment and support, so:

- Publish the quality being achieved. This will help your team understand how they are doing and how important it is that the standards are achieved.

- Meet regularly with your staff to discuss the quality being achieved as well as the vulnerabilities and priorities as they see them. Agree specific issues and action points for them to work on to improve quality. These may relate to:

  - training or coaching sessions
  - reviewing procedures or controls
  - improving documentation of checklists or procedures
  - discussing issues with clients.

Ask for an Audit

- Encourage ideas for improvements from your staff and consider introducing short-term suggestion schemes.

- Keep your boss posted on what you're doing on quality and this might also generate more ideas and suggestions for improvement.

Address key vulnerabilities early

Tackle vulnerabilities which may lead to problems in achieving your standards. Your information systems should have detected these, and your job is to ensure that any significant problems are removed or reduced. You need to:

- **Understand the problem**

  Ask yourself:

  - what is the impact?
  - what is the scale?
  - who is affected?
  - what is the cost to the Company (in money or reputation)?
  - what is the cause?

  You may need to assign someone to investigate the problem further, for example by extra sampling of work or discussing it with other people.

- **Document the problem**

  Briefly summarise what the problem is in writing, including what is the impact and what is the cause. This helps you clarify things in your own mind and helps communicate the issue to others.

- **Discuss alternative solutions**

  For larger problems involve people from other affected areas and from specialist areas such as Audit and Controls or Business Systems.

- **Decide on the appropriate action**

  Analyse the alternative solutions and cost them. Weigh up the benefits and costs of each and make a decision in the best interests of the Company. Remember that it may be the right decision to live with a vulnerability if the costs of a complete solution are too high.

Develop the right approach

Encourage these key beliefs on Quality:

- It is possible to achieve the quality standards all the time.

- It is always less expensive to do the work right first time.

- Keeping procedures simple helps achieve standards.

- Paying attention to detail helps achieve the quality required. Your people really need to care about small details.

- Question everything. Why do things this way or why do them at all?

- If you can see a problem relating to a colleague or another department, don't ignore it. Raise it constructively. Everyone has an interest in quality.

Managing Quality

Set Clear Standards

- Consult your customers
- Decide on appropriate quality standards
- Communicate quality standards
- Review these standards

Achieve the Standards Required

- Establish the procedures and methods
- Determine and implement controls
- Agree responsibility for quality
- Write up and action training plans

Quality Assurance

Track the Quality Achieved

- Install quality controls
- Sound out your customers
- Discuss quality with your staff
- Ask for an audit

Quality Control

Improve Quality

- Involve your staff
- Address key vulnerabilities early
- Develop the right approach

12 MANAGING PRODUCTIVITY

As a Manager you are responsible for the productivity of your area. To understand what this means and achieve results, you need to:

- Focus on productivity
- Plan to be productive
- Ensure performance is productive
- Maximise productivity.

Focus on productivity

The starting point is for you and your people to understand what is meant by productivity and why it is important. Sharpening everyone's focus is the first step to improvement.

Understand what productivity means

Think about and explain to everyone what productivity means in your area.

In general terms productivity is about getting value for money out of what we invest in people, machines, and other resources. It is a measure of OUTPUT compared with INPUT.

INPUT is the sum of all costs associated with any activity – people costs, furniture costs, equipment costs, stationery costs, etc.

OUTPUT is the completed job and will vary according to the function, for example the number of policies issued, the number of lines of coding completed, etc.

What are the inputs and outputs in your area? When you know that, your objective is to increase the amount of output for a given level of input, or alternatively reduce the level of input for a given level of output.

Explain why productivity is important

Your people need to understand what productivity means and how important it is. One vital element of that message is that productivity is not necessarily about working harder or longer, but about using resources better. It's really about working smarter!

The reason we all need to go on improving productivity is to keep ahead in increasingly competitive markets. Improved productivity leads to improved profitability which in turn leads to:

- more keenly priced products
- better value for our clients
- job security, good rewards and a share of success for all employees.

So productivity is vital to everyone associated with your business. Explain why it is important to your staff and show that we all need to be committed to improve.

Aim for effectiveness

Effectiveness means doing the right things.

Check whether your area is effective. Before undertaking any new piece of work, the most important questions to ask are:

- Why are we doing this?
- Is what we are about to do really necessary?

- Will the cost of doing it give a worthwhile return on the investment?

Ask these same questions regularly about long established practices. Keep challenging the status quo as things which were done in the past may no longer be necessary. The other aspect of effectiveness is deciding what to do first. Sometimes – particularly in a project environment – you will be faced with conflicting priorities. For each, compare the value of the anticipated benefit with the cost of achieving it. You won't necessarily pick your top priority on purely financial grounds, but the approach will certainly help your decision.

Aim for efficiency

Efficiency means doing things in the right way. If it needs to be done, are we doing it in the most productive way possible? Even when you have decided what should be done, how, by whom, where and when, you should always be looking for a better way.

There are various techniques to help you do this, for example:

- Brainstorming to generate lots of ideas
- Flow charting to show the sequence of events. Where work moves from one place to another, check that the same work is not being done twice
- Work measurement to show how long a job takes
- Piloting or simulating to test whether new ideas will work.

The objective of all the techniques is the same:

- get as many ideas as possible
- sift through them to draw up a short list
- test the alternatives
- implement the best one.

Plan to be productive

Managing productivity requires a great deal of thought, and the only way to achieve results is to take time and prepare a proper plan. The plan is an estimate, or if possible a measure, of what work is to be done and the optimum resources needed to do it.

Assess your workload

Before undertaking any piece of work, assess how much effort is required and how long it will take. Produce a plan of the overall workload for the period under review. The key elements in assessing the workload are:

- how long does it take to do the job once?

- how many times will you need to do it?

To help with analysis, break the work down into measurable tasks, measure each task separately, and build up the individual measurements to form the complete picture.

Wherever possible, use a work measurement technique to estimate the effort needed to deliver the expected workload.

The frequency of planning will vary according to circumstances but as a minimum you would normally expect to set and review your workload plan at least twice a year and more frequently in a changing situation.

Staff correctly

Using your projected workload estimates, you can then calculate the number of people needed to do the work.

It may be that the staffing requirement varies from month to month or even from week to week. For one-off peaks you should plan to use overtime or temporary staff, or for work which is not time-critical, allow temporary backlogs to build up.

Assess Your Workload

Provide the right tools for the job

You can also influence productivity by the facilities you provide to do the job. Here are examples of things to think about and plan:

- **Office Layout**

  Position your people and equipment to make the flow of work as streamlined as possible:

  - Where possible, group together people carrying out different stages of a single job.
  - Site common facilities to make them as accessible as possible to their users.
  - Decide whether the work is best accomplished by providing privacy for your staff or an open layout which makes communication and movement easier.

- **Equipment**

  Agree who needs what equipment to do their job, and make use of any available facilities which reduce the overall cost of delivering the end product of your section. Where equipment is available, make sure that people are trained to get the maximum use out of it. Here are some examples:

  - *Dictating machines.* Dictation is far quicker than hand-writing. Train and encourage your staff to use it.

  - *Calculators.* Different models are available which can handle anything from simple arithmetic to complex mathematical formulae. Some machines provide just a visual display of the calculation while others provide a hard-copy record of the stages of calculation. Pick the ones suitable to the work of your area.

  - *Word processing.* WP equipment makes it possible to store standard letters and reports, and build in variables suitable to the occasion.

- *Computers*. High volume processes are usually best handled by computers. If you need guidance, seek help in comparing the cost of developing and running a computer system with existing manual procedures.

- *Telephones*. It is worth spending time getting to understand and use the facilities available.

- **Paperwork**

  Think through the possible options for streamlining your procedures and providing the right documentation to support them.

  - *Forms*. If a procedure is repeated frequently, a form is a useful vehicle for presenting standard information and guiding people through the steps they need to follow.

  - *Written procedures*. Writing down the steps in each process ensures that there are no gaps, aids consistency of practice and is useful to support on-the-job-training.

  - *Worksheets, progress sheets and checklists*. Internal documents which remind people of the steps to be followed or provide a record of the process can be useful to ensure the task is carried out in every respect.

  - *Tables*. If repetitive calculations need to be carried out, tables are a useful method of providing quick answers.

These are just examples – the list of possible aids to productivity is huge. The key objective is to compare the cost of using an extra facility with the cost of the time saved as a result of its use.

Schedule projects

Planning applies just as much to *ad hoc* project work as to ongoing processing. When faced with managing a project, the first question to ask is whether there is a specific deadline which must be met for external reasons. The imposition of an external deadline will determine the resources needed to achieve the project. If there is no specific deadline, estimate the alternative end dates of the project depending on the resources invested in it.

To make both estimation and execution easier, break the project down into individual tasks. Sometimes the order in which each task is carried out can be varied, sometimes there will be interdependencies between tasks with the results of one feeding into another. Develop a written schedule which with the resources being used enables the project to be completed:

- at least cost
- in the shortest time scale
- with the least risk of over-running
- with the best chance of producing an acceptable result.

Ensure performance is productive

Having planned for productivity you need to manage your resources on a day-to-day basis to ensure that you get the optimum use out of them. To help you do this, develop suitable productivity measures to track progress.

Manage your resources efficiently

To get the best value from your people, keep track of what work needs to be done, and adjust your plan as circumstances dictate:

- Balance the work-load of the sections/people under your control. Be flexible in moving people from less busy functions to more busy functions, or, if more appropriate, transfer work to areas with spare capacity.

- Co-ordinate holiday plans to ensure that cover is available for the key tasks which are your responsibility.

- Smooth the workflow to avoid bottlenecks because a peak of work at one stage of an operation will lead to waiting time at later stages.

- Defer recruitment where you can. Overtime provides a more flexible resource, provided you are not making excessive demands.

Establish productivity measures

Establish an appropriate method of measuring productivity. Use a consistent measure so that a valid comparison of productivity can be made between one period and another. Here are some examples:

- Establish the standard cost of doing an hour of work and then compare that with the total cost of the staff resources (including management) actually used to deliver that hour of work.

- Use Full Time Equivalent (FTE) staffing. Compare actual staff resources used against your plan. The FTE measure converts all hours paid for (including overtime, temporary staff and part-time staff) into the equivalent number of Full Time Staff who would be needed to do the work.

- From time to time, you will need a measure which gives you the total cost of delivering a definable amount of work. For example, by comparing the costs in people, computer systems and other resources for a job done in two different ways, you can decide whether to change methods or extend automation further.

Track levels of productivity

Having determined your productivity measures, track progress against your plan. Frequency may vary but you should

Track Levels of Productivity

aim to do this at least once a month. Is the volume as anticipated? Is the effort expended in doing the work as anticipated?

If there is a variation from the plan, you need to decide whether this means that something is going wrong and you need to make changes to get back on course or alternatively whether the plan was wrong, in which case you need to make adjustments.

Similarly, with projects, keep track of progress against target and identify any slippage or potential slippage so that you can take action to get back on track.

Maximise productivity

The ultimate objective of all your planning and tracking is to maximise productivity. Always try to get the full benefit from the resources you are responsible for.

Involve your people

Involve your people in striving to improve productivity.

- Publicise measures and targets for productivity. Show how your team is doing against target on a monthly basis.

- Re-emphasise the importance of productivity and give credit or rewards to people who come up with good ideas.

- Always be open to suggestions and occasionally run campaigns, suggestion schemes or competitions.

- Encourage an open and questioning attitude amongst your people on the work that they do.

- Encourage two-way communication on productivity and make sure that everyone knows whether productivity is improving or the reverse.

- Lead by example. Show that you understand the value of time by being punctual and taking deadlines seriously.

Look for better ways

This is the constant challenge. Continually direct your efforts and those of your people towards improving productivity:

- Don't be complacent. There is always a better way, if only you can find it.

- Challenge the established way of doing things and keep asking the dumb questions: Why, What, How, Who, Where, When?

- Respect intuition. Analysis is not always the most fruitful way of making progress, and over-analysis can lead to paralysis. There are lots of circumstances where the best way of finding out whether an alternative works is to try it on a pilot basis and compare results.

Reduce costs

Keep up the pressure for everyone to be cost-conscious and avoid waste. We all have a part to play here – these are just a few examples:

- Maintain appropriate stock levels of stationery and printed matter.

- Circulate non-critical items rather than copying them.

- Let people know when you can be removed from a distribution list.

- If an external telephone call can wait until afternoon, take advantage of the fact that it's cheaper then.

- Don't have more furniture and office space than you need.

In summary, think about how costs are incurred and ways of reducing them. Encourage your staff to do the same.

Seek Outside Help

Seek outside help

Other departments can provide professional help and guidance to help you maximise your productivity, and if you think that such help could achieve results, make use of the services offered by others like Systems, Finance and Audit.

Very often an external review can prove a really effective way of improving productivity. Try the 'Man from Mars' approach. Use help from another Division or one of the specialist functions. You have everything to gain!

Checklist 12

Managing Productivity

Focus on Productivity

- Understand what productivity means
- Explain why productivity is important
- Aim for effectiveness
- Aim for efficiency

Plan to be Productive

- Assess your workload
- Staff correctly
- Provide the right tools for the job
- Schedule projects

Ensure Performance is Productive

- Manage your resources efficiently
- Establish productivity measures
- Track levels of productivity

Maximise Productivity

- Involve your people
- Look for better ways
- Reduce costs
- Seek outside help

Index

absenteeism 112
accessibility 29-30, 101-102, 104
accountability 11, 29, 107, 108, 119
action points 47
advertising 68, 92
Advisory, Conciliation and Arbitration Service (ACAS) 58
agendas 104
assessment
    communication 100-101
    cost effectiveness 137
    performance 51, 53
    productivity 136-137, 139
    staffing levels 132
    training 86, 88
    workload 132
auditors 124, 126, 142
authorisation procedures 122

benefits (see salary)
boss
    communication with 2, 4, 6, 35, 37-38, 42, 53, 54, 57, 59, 63, 64, 79, 93, 99, 100, 119, 126
brainstorming 131
business systems analysts 126

calculators 134
calmness 19
caring 6, 23, 25-27
chains of command 4, 29-30, 107-108, 113
chairmanship of meetings 104
checklists 83, 122, 124, 135
checkpoint meetings 29, 122
circulation lists 140
clients (see customers)
coaching 50, 82, 85-86, 124

communication (see also meetings)
    accessibility of manager 29-30, 101-102, 104
    as key management activity 6
    assessment 100-101
    basic skills 95-96
    basic techniques 19, 21-22
    distribution lists 9, 99
    documentation 104
    establishment of system 99-101
    notice boards 99
    planning 104
    with boss 2, 4, 6, 35, 37-38, 42, 53, 54, 57, 59, 63, 64, 79, 93, 99, 100, 119, 126
    with customers 108, 119-120, 122, 123, 124
    with other managers 2, 53, 79, 93, 99, 108
    with specialist managers 67, 77, 78, 79, 93, 124, 126, 142
    with staff 2, 6, 25, 44-45, 47, 49-51, 53, 54, 64, 68, 85, 88-89, 99-102, 104, 120, 122, 123, 124, 126, 131, 139-40
competition 110
computers 135, 137
confidentiality 72, 78, 100
consideration 23, 25-27, 69, 71-73
consistency 21-22
consultation (see communication)
copies lists 9
corporate approach 18
cost effectiveness 113, 130-131, 137, 140
counselling 82
courses 82, 86
courtesy 23, 25
criticism 47, 49, 83
cross-training 90
customers 108, 119-20, 122, 123, 124

deadlines 136
decision-making 6, 28-29, 120
delegation
    as key management activity 6, 11, 13-14, 34
    in teamwork 110
    motivation of staff 13, 50
    to secretary 11

demotion 53
dependability 22
development (see also training)
    as key management activity 5
    communication with staff 88-89
    job design 90
    planning 90, 92-93
    policy 81, 88
diaries 7, 10, 11, 99
discipline
    communication with boss 57, 59
    documentation 62
    interviews 59-60, 62, 63
    planning 59
    policy 53, 57-58
    procedures 53, 58-60, 62-63
    standards of conduct 58
discretion 22
dismissal 53-58, 59
distribution lists 9, 99
documentation (see also lists)
documentation (see also paperwork)
documentation (see also writing)
    communications 104
    disciplinary procedures 62
    performance management 45, 53
    productivity management 135
    quality management 120, 122, 123, 124, 126
    training management 82
'dumping'
    information 100
    staff 92
    work 11

evaluation (see assessment, job evaluation)

fairness 21-22, 57-58, 75, 76, 78
favouritism 22
feedback (see communication)
filing systems 9-10, 46-47
finance officers 142

flexibility
  allocation of workload 136-137
  organisation 107
  staffing 115-116
flow charts 131
forms 135
full time equivalent (FTE) 137

goals (see objectives)
grading 75, 77
grievances
  avoidance 23, 63-64
  communication
    with boss 57, 63, 64
    with staff 64
  procedures 63-64
'growing your own' 90, 92

'halo effect' 78
hard work 18
helping out 19
hierarchy (see chains of command)
holidays 116, 137
humanity 21

individual training plans 82
induction 82, 83-84
information systems 46
instruction 84-85
interviews 59-60, 62-63, 68, 69, 71-72

job descriptions 4, 14, 45, 67, 68, 77, 122
job design 90, 113
job evaluation 75, 77, 78, 79
job specification 67-68
'jurisdiction' of manager over staff 58

leadership 17-19, 27-30, 109-10, 139
levels of management 107
levels of supervision 49-50
liaison meetings 99

listening 97
lists (see also paperwork)
10, 44, 47, 83, 99, 122, 124, 135, 140

'macho' management style 58
mail 10
management techniques
caring and consideration 23, 25-27
cultivation of good working relationships 19, 21-22
leadership 17-19, 27-30, 109-110, 139
maximisation of results 27-30
manager's self-management
delegation 11, 13-14
effectiveness 2, 4-7
efficiency 7, 9-11
evaluation of performance 1-2
motivation 5
positive attitude 18, 83, 84, 85
presentation 9, 95-96
medical reports 73
meetings (see also communication)
29, 44, 46-47, 99, 104, 122
memoranda 9, 96
monitoring 41, 45-47
morale 112
motivation
as key management activity 5
of manager 5
of staff 13, 25, 42, 44, 47, 49, 50, 83, 112, 120

naturalness 21
new posts 90
'no surprises' management 21, 35
note taking 10
notice boards 99

objectives
leadership 27-30
manager's performance 1-2, 4, 27-30
staff performance 41-42, 44-45
teamwork 109

training 82, 88
objectivity 78-79
office equipment 134-135
office layout 134, 140
openness 26, 35, 102
organisation
    as key management activity 6
    chains of command 4, 29-30, 107-108, 113
    cost effectiveness 113
    development of appropriate structure 107-108
    flexibility in staffing 115-116
    job design 90, 113
    measurement of effectiveness 112
    rationalisation 113
    spans of control 107-108
    specialisation 113
    teamwork 109-10
    time management 112
organisation charts 4
overtime 78, 132, 137

paperwork (see also lists)
    7, 9-11, 46-47, 99, 104, 122, 131, 135, 140
pay (see salary)
performance
    assessment 51-53
    communication
        with boss 35, 53
        with specialist managers 53
        with staff 44-45, 49-51, 53, 54
    documentation 45, 53
    maximisation 47, 49-51, 53-54
    monitoring 45-47
    motivation of staff 47, 49, 50
    objectives 41-42, 44-45
    organisation 110, 112-113, 115-116
    planning 41-42, 44-45, 115-116
    standards 28, 44, 47-49
    time management 44
performance appraisal 51, 53
performance plans 41, 44-45, 47

person specifications 67-68
personnel managers 67, 77, 78, 79, 93
piloting 131, 140
planning
    as key management activity 6
    communications management 104
    development of staff 90, 92-93
    disciplinary procedures 59-60
    performance management 41-42, 44-45, 115-116
    productivity management 132, 134-136, 137, 139
    quality management 119, 123
    succession of staff 115
    training of staff 81-82, 86
poor performance 49, 50, 53-54
positive attitude 18, 83, 84, 85
positive management 17
post (see mail)
praise (see recognition)
prejudices 22, 59
prioritisation 4, 28, 131
problem-solving 29
productivity
    communication
        with specialist managers 142
        with staff 139-140
    cost effectiveness 130-131, 137, 140
    definition 129-130
    documentation 135
    efficiency 131, 136-137
    importance 130, 139
    maximisation 139-140, 142
    measurement 136-137, 139
    office equipment 134-135
    office layout 134, 140
    paperwork 135
    planning 132, 134-136, 137, 139
    prioritisation 131
  staffing levels 132
  time management 135-136, 140
progress meetings 29, 44, 46-47
progress sheets 135

promotion 77

quality
  assurance 123
  communication
    with boss 119, 126
    with customers 119-120, 122, 123, 124
    with specialist managers 124, 126
    with staff 120, 122, 123, 124, 126
  control 119, 122, 123, 124
  different degrees 120
  documentation 120, 122, 123, 124, 126
  maximisation 118-20, 119, 124, 126-127
  planning 119, 123
  policy 127
  standards 112, 114-15, 119-120, 122-123, 127
  time management 120
  training 123, 124

rationalisation 113
recognition (see also salary)
  as key management activity 5
  policy 75, 78-79
  staff performance 14, 25-26, 30, 47, 49-50, 75, 77-78, 139
recruitment
  advertising 68
  alternative use of overtime 137
  communication with staff 68
  consideration for candidates 69, 71-73
  determination of needs 67-68
  interviews 68, 69, 71-72
  job offers 72-73
  medical reports 73
  practical exercises 71
  references 73
  standards 28, 67
  starting salary 73
  testing 71
  training 69
registers 122
reliability 22

reorganisation 113
resourcing 6
responsibility 19
reward (see recognition, salary)
rotation 82, 90

salary 73, 75, 77-78 (see also recognition)
salary reviews 73
secretary 10-11
self-awareness (see manager's self-management)
sense of humour 19
sickness 116
simulation 131
sincerity 22, 23-24
'sixth' sense for trouble 63
spans of control 107-108
specialisation 113
staff
  absenteeism 112
  communication with 2, 6, 25, 44-45, 47, 49-51, 53, 54, 64, 68,
      85, 88-89, 99-102, 104, 120, 122, 123, 124, 126, 131, 139-140
  development 81, 88-90, 92-93
  disciplinary procedures 53, 58-60, 62-63
  flexibility 115-16
  'growing your own' 90, 92, 115
  medical reports 73
  motivation 13, 25, 42, 44, 47, 49, 50, 82, 83, 112, 120
  new posts 90
  poor performance 49, 50, 53, 54
  overtime 78, 132, 137
  promotion 77
  provision of opportunities 89-90, 92-93
  recognition of performance 14, 25-26, 30, 47, 49-50, 75, 77-78,
      139
  recruitment 28, 67-69, 71-73, 137
  rotation 82, 90
  salary 73, 75, 77-78
  sickness 116
  succession 92-93, 115
  temporary 132
  training 50, 69, 81-86, 88, 90, 123-124

transfers 92-93
turnover 112, 116
standards
  conduct of staff 58
  hard work 18
  performance 28, 45, 47, 49
  quality 119-120, 122-123, 127
  recruitment 28, 67
succession 92, 93, 115
summary of management essentials
  boss 39
  communication 105
  development 94
  discipline 65
  grievances 65
  organisation 117
  performance 55
  productivity 143
  quality 128
  recruitment 74
  reward 80
  self 15
  staff 32-33
  training 94
systems analysts 142

targets 44, 45, 135-136, 139
teamwork 26, 38, 101, 109-110, 122
telephones 9, 10, 72, 135, 140
testing 71
time management 5, 7, 9, 44, 112, 120, 135-136, 139
'to do' lists 7, 10
training (see also development)
  assessment 86, 88
  coaching 50, 82, 85-86, 124
  counselling 82
  courses 82, 86
  documentation 82
  induction 83-84
  instruction 84-85
  job rotation 82, 90

motivation of staff 83-84
objectives 81, 88
on-the-job 82, 85
planning 81-82, 86
policy 81-82
quality management 123, 124
recruitment 69
transfers 92-93
trustworthiness 22-23
turnover 112, 116

'walking the job' 102, 104
warnings 57-60, 62
weekly copies system 46
word processing 134
workload
allocation 136-137
assessment 132
balance between doing and managing 4-5
balance between people-oriented and task-oriented
activities 5-6, 42
division between manager and boss 35, 37-38
measurement 131, 132
workload hour 137
worksheets 135
writing (see also documentation)
9, 10, 96